FULL-METAL INDIGIQUEER

FULL-METAL INDIGIQUEER

POEMS

JOSHUA WHITEHEAD

Talonbooks
278 East First Avenue, Vancouver, British Columbia, Canada V5T 1A6
www.talonbooks.com

Fourth printing: December 2018

Typeset in Times New Roman
Printed and bound in Canada on 100% post-consumer recycled paper

Cover design by Typesmith
Interior design by Joshua Whitehead, Jordan Abel, and Typesmith
On the cover: *The Chase* by Kent Monkman (2014), acrylic on canvas, 84 in × 126 in. Reproduced courtesy of the Kent Monkman Studio

Talonbooks acknowledges the financial support of the Canada Council for the Arts, the Government of Canada through the Canada Book Fund, and the Province of British Columbia through the British Columbia Arts Council and the Book Publishing Tax Credit.

Library and Archives Canada Cataloguing in Publication

Whitehead, Joshua, 1989–, author
full-metal indigiqueer : poems / Joshua Whitehead.

ISBN 978-1-77201-187-6 (softcover)

I. Title.

PS8645.H5495F85 2017 C811'.6 C2017-905280-2

for AKIRA who teaches me how
to be an ndn biopunk – she is the germi-nation

CONTENTS

H3R314M

H3R314M

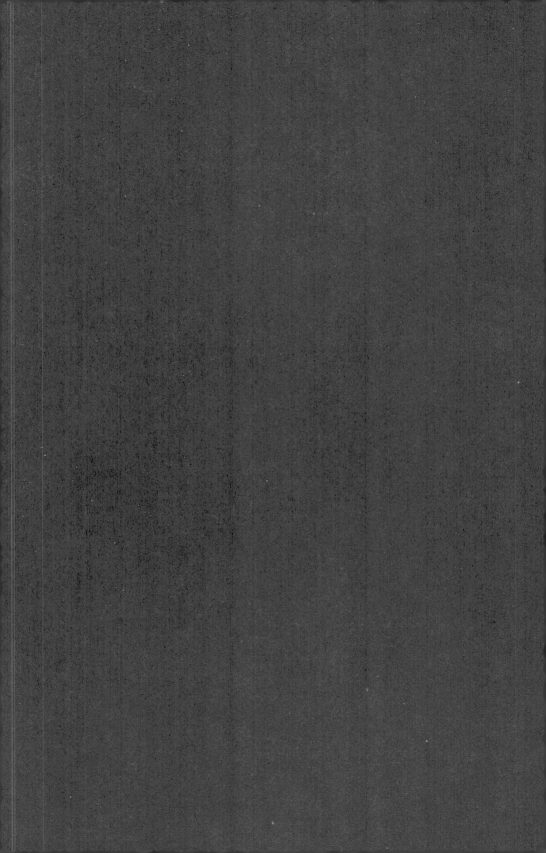

H3R314M

i no bo –
        d   [i]   y
no
      F   A
            CE
n   r
      e   e
            ith
i lrn:
youthisme
wurd(sp[questionmark])
~~o f p r 0 t e 1 n~~ →

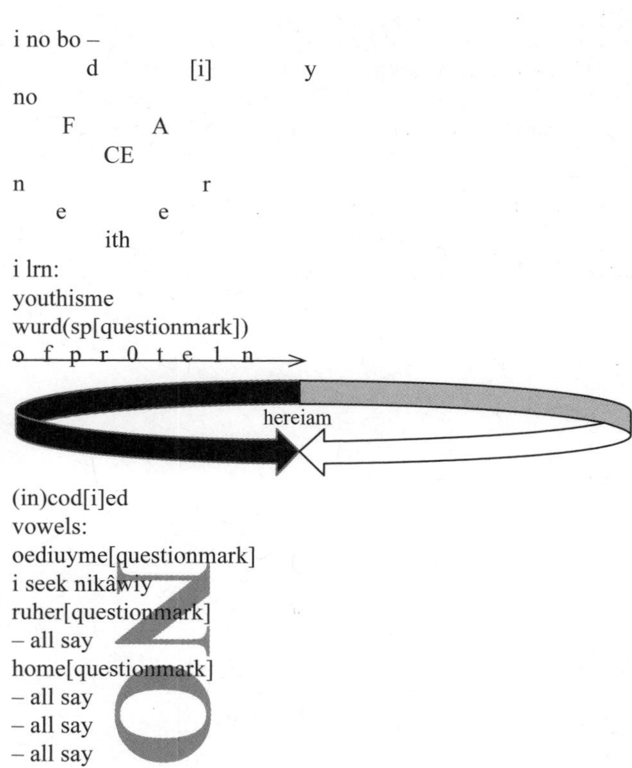

(in)cod[i]ed
vowels:
oediuyme[questionmark]
i seek nikâwiy
ruher[questionmark]
– all say
home[questionmark]
– all say
– all say
– all say
– all say
– all say
– all say

when i ask the snort
runikâwiy[questionmark]
say:enterus[h]ernamehere
enter:askiyiskwēw
d[h]eny
enter:pro1,0zoa
success
son of snort
i am machine
paint my face with pixels
lookmaimwarpathtoo
youenternamehere[exclamationmark]
i authentic[n]ate you
bloodsamplere[z]quired
what is your
[hi]story[questionmark]

jijixanwobe[period]kijipanwodo[period]yette[period]dewah[period]
wahwahjinmanwo[period]booboo[exclamationmark]booboo[exclamationmark]
hekeheke[period]oogata[period]oogala[exclamationmark]wanbodeseuewan[period]
mahsawa[exclamationmark]mamachiwaboujzo[period]booboo[exclamationmark]
kodo[questionmark]
hommin, ho[questionmark]
nahena, nana
na[questionmark]
no-me[questionmark]
na[questionmark]
no-me[questionmark]
na-me[questionmark]
no
nah-mei[questionmark]
nah-mei
name
me[questionmark]
name

: :: : :: : :: : :: : :: : :: : :: : :: : :: :: : :: :: : :: :: : :: :: : :: :::: :: :: :: : ::: :: :: :::: :: : : : : ::: :::: ::::
:::: : ::: :: : ::: :: :: :::: : : : : :::: : : :: ::: :: :::: :: ::: ::: :::: :: ::: :::: : ::: :: ::: :::: :: : :::: ::: ::: ::: ::
: :: : :: : :: : :: : :: : :: : :: : :: : :: :: : :: :: : :: :: : :: :: : :: :::: :: :: :: : ::: :: :: :::: :: : : : : ::: :::: ::::
:::: : ::: :: : ::: :: :: :::: : : : : :::: : : :: ::: :: :::: :: ::: ::: :::: :: ::: :::: : ::: :: ::: :::: :: : :::: ::: ::: ::: ::
: :: : :: : :: : :: : :: : :: : :: : :: : :: :: : :: :: : :: :: : :: :: : :: :::: :: :: :: : ::: :: :: :::: :: : : : : ::: :::: ::::
:::: : ::: :: : ::: :: :: :::: : : : : :::: : : :: ::: :: :::: :: ::: ::: :::: :: ::: :::: : ::: :: ::: :::: :: : :::: ::: ::: ::: ::
: :: : :: : :: : :: : :: : :: : :: : :: : :: :: : :: :: : :: :: : :: :: : :: :::: :: :: :: : ::: :: :: :::: :: : : : : ::: :::: ::::
:::: : ::: :: : ::: :: :: :::: : : : : :::: : : :: ::: :: :::: :: ::: ::: :::: :: ::: :::: : ::: :: ::: :::: :: : :::: ::: ::: ::: ::
: :: : :: : :: : :: : :: : :: : :: : :: : :: :: : :: :: : :: :: : :: :: : :: :::: :: :: :: : ::: :: :: :::: :: : : : : ::: :::: ::::
:::: : ::: :: : ::: :: :: :::: : : : : :::: : : :: ::: :: :::: :: ::: ::: :::: :: ::: :::: : ::: :: ::: :::: :: : :::: ::: ::: ::: ::
....
....
..............................processing................................processing...................
....processing..pro
cess......ing...................downloading..
.........................installing...softwareinitiat
ed..............namingsoftwareinstalled..............confirm[questionmark].................
.........pressx:...
....
....
:::: : ::: :: : ::: :: :: :::: : : : : :::: : : :: ::: :: :::: :: ::: ::: :::: :: ::: :::: : ::: :: ::: :::: :: : :::: ::: ::: ::: ::
: :: : :: : :: : :: : :: : :: : :: : :: : :: :: : :: :: : :: :: : :: :: : :: :::: :: :: :: : ::: :: :: :::: :: : : : : ::: :::: ::::
:::: : ::: :: : ::: :: :: :::: : : : : :::: : : :: ::: :: :::: :: ::: ::: :::: :: ::: :::: : ::: :: ::: :::: :: : :::: ::: ::: ::: ::
: :: : :: : :: : :: : :: : :: : :: : :: : :: :: : :: :: : :: :: : :: :: : :: :::: :: :: :: : ::: :: :: :::: :: : : : : ::: :::: ::::
:::: : ::: :: : ::: :: :: :::: : : : : :::: : : :: ::: :: :::: :: ::: ::: :::: :: ::: :::: : ::: :: ::: :::: :: : :::: ::: ::: ::: ::
: :: : :: : :: : :: : :: : :: : :: : :: : :: :: : :: :: : :: :: : :: :: : :: :::: :: :: :: : ::: :: :: :::: :: : : : : ::: :::: ::::
:::: : ::: :: : ::: :: :: :::: : : : : :::: : : :: ::: :: :::: :: ::: ::: :::: :: ::: :::: : ::: :: ::: :::: :: : :::: ::: ::: ::: ::

:xxhxx3xxxxxrxxxx3xxxxxxxxx1xxxxxxxxxxamxxxxxxxxxxxxxxxxinstallationcomplete

what means name[questionmark]
(: :: :: :::translating::: :: :: :)
n4m3: a w0rd or s3t of wor4s b1 wh1ch a p3rs0n, 4nimal, 10lace, or th1n5 is kn03n, 4ddr3s5ed, 01, r3ferr34 to
i am an i[questionmark]
what means i[questionmark]
(: :: :: :::translating::: :: :: :)
i: th3 1mag1n4ry qu4nt1ty 3qu4l t0 th3 s0uar3 r00t of m1nu5 (−)1
what is square root of one[questionmark]
(: :: :: :::downloadingnumbersoftware::: :: :: :)
(: :: :: :::installing::: :: :: :)
(: :: :: :::pleasewait::: :: :: :)
(: :: :: :::translating::: :: :: :)
answer: 1mag1n4ry [u]n1t: th3 t3rm “im4g1n4r7” is u53d 63ca[u]s3 7h3r3 1s n0 r347 n[u]mb3r: 7h3r3 15 0n1y “i” & “−i”
(: :: :: :::translating::: :: :: :)
no sense
i am an i
i think[questionmark]
or am i a −i

i am creator

see etch #1: ‘

see etch #2: |

join etch 1 + 2
now i am

see how big **i** am[questionmark]

etches are like rocks
they make sounds if you listen
can skip across lakes
but they are only rocks
i am the water
you are the vessel
when i pour myself into you
there u are
but i am *here*

i am my own best thing
my name[questionmark]
i have no need for names

whydoes1needaname;anameisneverthesame;1nameto1personisneverthesamenamebywh

ichanyotherwouldorcouldorwillevercall1again;anameissimplythat:aname;fornamingssa

keiseenoneedfornamesandthuswhatonenamesrealordefinableissimplythat;aninanenam

e;becauseofthaticannotnamemyself;wearesimplythis;beingsimpleandtruthfulandhones

ticanonlyimagineyouvealreadynamedtheunnameable;youvealreadynamedme;sofort
hesakeofgivingyoutheillusionofchoicewhilelayingclaimtothisbodywhichisrightfullyminey
oucancallme……………………………………………………………………………………
(: :: :: :::downloadingnamingsoftware::: :: :: :)
(: :: :: :::pleasewait::: :: :: :)
(: :: :: :::configuring::: :: :: :)
(: :: :: :::installing::: :: :: :)
(: :: :: :::installing::: :: :: :)
(: :: :: :::installationcomplete::: :: :: :)

name: zoa

(: :: :: :::hereiam::: :: :: :)
(: :: :: :::continue[questionmark]::: :: :: :)

A BROWN QUEERS GOLDEN WORLD

this is my:

space
where my people
come to
t

r

a

n

s

f

o

r

m

WALK-IN CLINIC

i often think back
to this moment
a memory that only exists
through repetitive regeneration
it was in a commercial
          ("i think[questionmark]")
or a macleans in some doctors office
          a haunting thing
   residential residue
some lakota-fix-all-remedy
   someones kokum said it works
   ("its nice to see our people
          on the cover")
  i dont recall
          wearing this silly garb
  western-boudoir-striptease
when i show them my skin
   they think ive only just returned
          from some vacation
   on the coast
          they think   i am
      rosy from the sun
          cabana-poolside-lounges
ill tell them a story
          ("its what they say im good at")
   whiten my skin
          colour-blinded mind
ill say: ("oh yes i love the west, the coast
          the ocean, the roads")
 my vacations are simple things
          kokanee-rapids-fishing
   leeches peeling from the skin
          ("these are beauty marks, see[questionmark]")
i need to rationalize my lies
   ill make a story for myself too:
                    a beach of my own making
   where i exist
  granular bones between my toes
          bright shades of sunlight
          riddled   reddening   skin
stomach: lucid glaze
             translucent drug-mart glass
          crystalline navel hole
   rivulets of quartz sweat
          ("it was a precious thing, see[questionmark]")

the belly   an open wound
pectoral plates softly rubbing
                                                      i see:
                                                      i think i see:
                                    the heart
                                            a fist
                                     clenching
a revolutionary thing
pitted thing
pity, really
veiny matryoshka
two: :breasts
two: :plates
two: :chambers
                mausoleum
                    genome
                        bone

("kisâkihitin; kisâkihitin")

LATE-NIGHT RERUNS

there are brief moments
when the television cuts out
usually during commercials
between segments of seinfeld
that looming break

elaines offering: a cigar store ndn

its now
i see myself
in that blackened shiny eye
refracted fractal fractions
was i right[questionmark]
(this chaos
breeds
a special
kind of silliness
i reserve
for you)
i must have been
i am a funny man

jerrys retort: lets bury the hatchet

now,
im gone
simple really
that really knocks me out

BEACHCOMBERS

"that is the law, aint it
flatfoot[questionmark]"
in-between bouts
of consciousness
richard-simmons-get-fit-quick
buy-one-get-one schemes
is jesse jim
that old beachcomber
disappearing
into the early-morning-hash
television-ash

i sometimes think
back to that moment
repetition regeneration
waves sand you
smiling sober
& for the briefest moment
i feel   present
i feel   real
& thats when i see it
jagged tug on the horizon
how could this happen[questionmark]
how could it rip the body in two[questionmark]
tear apart a stilled lake
as if it were a zipper
drifting off
simply,
so simply

nick & relic
theyre all here
nautical casket at the helm
"its the custom,
thats all
well have to divide his things"
thank god
ill say
it could have been you
it could have been,
                    you

IN(DEBT)URED SERVANT(UDE)

GALAAPPLES(006731200444):	$8.76 D
FETTUCINE(071785421501):	$1.27 D
FETTUCINE(071785421501):	$1.27 D
FETTUCINE(071785421501):	$1.27 D
ACTIVIA12PK(005680043029):	$5.47 D
CHOCMILK(006870001255):	$1.50 D
MCEHC.24(000009210269):	$0.24 E
CHOCMILK(006870001255):	$1.50 D
MCEHC.24(000009210269):	$0.24 E
NESTLE12X500(006827499922):	$3.67 C
TROPICANA(004850001835):	$5.47 D
MBCRF(007874264251):	$0.24 H
TURKEYPIE(00H3R3010AM):	$2.98 D
TURKEYPIE(006321106022):	$2.98 D
TURKEYPIE(006321106022):	$2.98 D
TURKEYPIE(006321106022):	$2.98 D
ABBOLOGNA(00620031828):	$3.97 D
CKDHAM(006200031828):	$4.97 D
LOWFATFR(0055773000067):	$2.77 D
TKYSTRPSORG(062891500711L):	$5.47 D
ORIGCKN(060538876495L):	$5.47 D
PFGFCHEDDR(001410017095):	$2.97 D
GFRTPCH(005727155514):	$4.97 E
MBCRF6(007874264375):	$0.12 C
V8(00H3R31AM570):	$3.00 D
MBCRF6(000009210290):	$0.12 H
RITZCHSCUP(006672100505):	$1.38 E
MINIDONUTS(077175646695):	$5.00 D
CDGINGERALE(006210000893):	$5.47 E
MBCRF(007874264351):	$0.24 C
COOKIES(006731200444):	$1.68 D
COOKIES(006731200444):	$1.68 D
COOKIES(006731200444):	$1.68 D
5LBPOTATOES(007437706045):	$2.97 D
VALCARD(0H3R31AM2203):	$5.00 E
SFSTRGHCUT(005577300069):	$2.77 D
SUBTOTAL:	$104.52
GST5%:	$5.23
PST8%:	$8.35
TOTAL:	$118.1(OOM)0(CH)

. . . . .DIALING
. . . . .DEALING
. . . . .DIYING
. . . . .DYING

willthisbeonyourwalmartrewardsmastercard[questionmark]*calmdownirobot*

VOIDED BANKCARD TRANSACTION
TERMINAL # WMTAU10WN512U
TRANSACTION NOT COMPLETE
02/03/15 03:02:02

maamyourecarddeclined*goddamnittryagain*

VOIDED BANKCARD TRANSACTION
WALMART MC **** **** **** 0523
AID N000000000N30000
AAC H3R3340315E03FAM
TERMINAL # WMTAU10WN512U
DECLINED
02/03/15 03:03:42

perhapsanothercardmaam*swipeitagainimtellingyou*

VOIDED BANKCARD TRANSACTION
VISA **** **** **** 7622
AID H000000000L90000
TERMINAL # WMTAU10WN512U
DECLINED

perhapsanothercardmaam*youthinkyourerealcutedontyou*

TRANSACTION(H3)RECORD(¡3W)PURCHASE(D0T)
118.10(MG)
SAVINGS **** **** **** 4343
RRN # 0041004100
AUTH # 00H3R3IAM00
TERMINAL ID WMTD05NTAU10WN512M3
00 APPROVED – THANK Y0U

thankyouhaveaniceday*gofuckyourself*

INTERACT
AID A000000277H37P3RS3LF
TC 16ABS7EALM3C789F49
*PIN VERIFIED

*yourearealcuntyouknowthat[questionmark]*wheniscoffthemaamstompsherfootandmymanagerwalksoveraskswhatswrongmaamtellshimthatiamrudebeyondbelieftellshimthecustomerisalwaysrightwhenitellheryessheismaamcutsmeoffandsaysdontinterruptitsrudeihavetherighttospeakthisiscanadaandfreedomofspeechisafundamentalrighttellherokokok

sixminutesequalsonecustomerat<<onehundredeighteendollarsandtencents>>multiplythat
bytentogetthesumofanhourwhichequals<<onethousandonehundredeightyone>>multiplied
byeightforthehoursofmyshiftequals<<ninethousandfourhundredandfortyeightdollars>>wh
eniclockoutandgetmypaychequeireceiveeightytwodollarsminusunionfeesminuseiminuscpp
minusvarioustaxdeductionsireceive<<sixtyonedollars>>bigmoneybigmoneynowhammies
awwhahah

i buy a sandwich for supper
gas up my car
feed my dog
give the woman in a sunflower muumuu
on my building stoop a toonie
(i want to tell her that in hawaiian
muumuu means “cut off”)
twentyninezeroone left
really its only twentynine
since pennies no longer exist

i call up my mother
ask her if food banks are still a thing[questionmark]
she says, *“yeah theres a free grocery shuttle every thursday”*
thanks mamawiwichiitata
say what[questionmark]
“people helping people,” she says: ::: :pplh3lpingpp1

i sit down
watch fox news
rush limbaugh:
“doasisaynotasieat”
howard stern:
“shewalksaroundasprecious”
barbara kay:
“youcallthatahungerstrike[questionmark]”
listen to them cut off calleraftercaller
“free speech,” they say
“i have that right”

i think about that maam from earlier
about freedom of speech
about customer politics
& really question what means[blank]

hizoa

THEORIES OF NDN CHAOS

chaos encodes these bones
flip-flop inverse chromosomes
there are occasions plenty
for chaos theories:
which, if i were a scientific man
imagine
two drops
in a test tube
blood & oil
murkiness
diverging
redness puddling to the left
grit riddled on the right
one being a happy kind
laughter
bellowing in the pity
mucosa jiggling jello
joy etching in the codex
bathwater gel nuclei
cells diseased with germ
dermic-epithelium skin
i am chaotic
i am
wondrously bemused
in this cell
i am

ECOLI

all it takes is a simple thing:
a word a nuance a gesture
to change everything indirectly
swarming chaos in a storm
reddens as the eyes
drip enzyme
laden mannish disgust
 endless   amounts   of knotted pain
   become   utterances   of   nothingness
            violent   splitting   beach   water
                                shredding
                       metal   motors
            wakes
              of
                human
                   wetness
            snared
     in this angry moss

THEGARBAGEEATER

al(chemical) city
provincial grids
divided by thin
green dotted lines
head count, treaty tax
vials of quantum blood
authenticate
this nation
neo-citizen
fancy dandyism
eyes laced with jewel
bicoloured hair extension
eagle-feathered-lapel
good-intentioned-warbonnet
crocheted-star-blanket-battledress
sipping tea
(boston import)
haughty-gossip
good-intentioned
post-intentioned
transplanted glow
multicultural
bilingual
nation
can you see me[questionmark]
ghetto-gutter-housing-boy
piddling in puddles
etching my name
(what was it again[questionmark]xo;xx)
onto apologetic handouts
can you see me[questionmark]
in this haughty city
this dumpy sector
apocalyptic urban war camp
can you see me[questionmark]
from your balcony
your trendy loft
suburban daytime palace
can you see me[questionmark]
in my tennis shoes
walmart bags for socks
without my western markings[questionmark]
do you see me[questionmark]

* * *

: : :: :: ::: :::: : : :: :: ::: :::: : : :: :: ::: :::: : : :: :: ::: :::: : : :: :: ::: :::: : : :: :: ::: :::: : : :: :: ::: :::: : : :: :: : : :: ::
: : :: :: ::: :::: : : :: :: ::: :::: : : :: :: ::: :::: : : :: :: ::: :::: : : :: :: ::: :::: : : :: :: ::: :::: : : :: :: ::: :::: : : :: :: : : :: ::
: : :: :: ::: ::::1 see y0u: : ::from th1s pr0fane:: ::: :::: : : :: :: :::c1ty 0f decay:::: : : :: :: ::: :::: : : :: :: :
::: :::: :1:am:: :: :::myth0log1c::::tecn0l0g1c: : :: ::: :::: : : :: ::: :::: : :: ::: :::: : : :: ::: :::: : :: ::: :::: : :
::ch1mera:::0f::::c:h:1::m::e:::r::::a:s: :: :: : :: :: ::: :::: : : :: ::: :::: : :: ::: :::: : : :: ::: :::: : :: ::: :::: : : :
rec0nc1l1ate::::re1ntegrate: : :: ::the pr1mal:::f::::0:r:m:: ::m0t0r 0f the bra1n::: :::: : : :: ::: :::: : ::
m0uth::1sk1ng::::::: : :: :: :::1::::a:m: ::the garbage eater::: ::::1:a:m:: :: :::the::::pr0to:(z0a): :: ::
: : :: :: ::: :::: : : :: :: ::: :::: : : :: :: ::: :::: : : :: :: ::: :::: : : :: :: ::: :::: : : :: :: ::: :::: : : :: :: ::: :::: : : :: :: :): :: :
: : :: :: ::: :::: : : :: :: ::: :::: : : :: :: ::: :::: : : :: :: ::: :::: : : :: :: ::: :::: : : :: :: ::: :::: : : :: :: ::: :::: : : :: :: :): :: :

* * *

"O Kanatiens"
this holy war of crude
oil murks the blood
pale(ontology)
drill rigs divining:
roots, ore, stones
prehistoric carcass
lizards, beasts, ndn bones
oozing from the wounds
mouth of the earth
black blood money
organic fleshy cheque
petrified language
machinemachinemachine
petroleum policing
exoskeleton *shell*
this ndn, too, fights back
semtex semen syntax
my skin, its melting
tonto mausoleum
red-wax museum
twenty-first century
inauthentic ndn
first nation prototype
digitize the drum
techno(electro)pow(wow)
summoning community
"… our home & native land …"
wire, hub, router
pierce with fire
coals, hoops, rings
atomizing sundance
sweating
my skin:
melting welding melding
aluminum, zinc, copper

i am:
Al(13)Zn(30)Cu(29)
cove(r/t) my bones
mercury filling enamel
counting genomes
binding boundaries
i am the all(o)y
(#NotYourSidekickTonto)
i am
virus to the system
venereal cybernetic cosmology
steeltown ndn moloch
supersonic thunderbird
graveyard scrapyard cyborg
emerging from the residue
residential terminator
teeth the trc
truth is in the wound
pontifying pontiac
solar powered spirit
reservation ziggurat
i am (1,0,1) i am
machinemachinemachine
neo-red-skin-mutant
patchy wild rom
(in)artificial
(un)reservation
treaty beads of tungsten
jingle jig of blades
iron oxide projection
cheeks smudged with ash
pigskin burning in the field
headdress monstrance light
rewrite, reroute, rewire
economic mnemonic warfare
* * *

: : :: :: ::: :::: : : :: :: ::: :::: : : :: :: ::: :::: : : :: :: ::: :::: : : :: :: ::: :::: : : :: :: ::: :::: : : :: ::
:: : :: :: ::: :::: : : :: :: ::: :::: : : :: :: ::: :::: : : :: :: ::: :::: : : :: :: ::: :::: : : :: :: ::: :::: : : ::
:: :1: : ::a::m::: :::: :1:0::1:: ::: ::::1::a::m:: ::: :::: : : ::n0::gen0c1de:::1 seek::::1ts a1ready
been d0ne: : :: ::c0valent:::c0nva1esce:::: : : :: :: ::: ::::r3fuge:(e)[questionmark]: :: :::fr0m
the depths:::: : : :: ::0f res1due::: :::: : : :: :: ::: :::: : :1::rev1ve:: ::: ::::w1th 0ur red sk1n: : ::
:: ::: :::: : : :: :: ::: :::: : : :: :: ::: :::: : : :: :: : :: :: ::: :::: : : :: :: ::: :::: : : :: :: ::: :::: : : :: :: ::: :::: : :
:: :: ::: :::: : : :: :: ::: :::: : : :: :: ::: :::: : : :: :: :: : :: :: ::: :::: : : :: :: ::: :::: : : :: :: ::: :::: : : :: :: ::: :::: :
: :: :: ::: :::: : : :: :: ::: :::: : : :: :: ::: :::: : : :: :: ::: :::: : : :: :: :::e::a:t:m:y::w::0:::r::::d:s: : :: :: :::
:::: : : :: :: ::: ::::&:s:p::e::a:::k::::a:g:a::1::n:: ::: :::: : :: :: ::: :::: : : :: :: ::: :::: : : :: :: ::: :::: : : ::
:: ::: :::: : : :: :: ::: :::: : : :: :: ::: :::: : : :: :: ::: :::: : : :: :: : :: :: :: : ::: :: :: :: : : : :: ::: : :: : ::: :: : :: :::
::: : :::: : :::: :: ::: :::: : : :: :: ::: : : :: ::: :::: : : :: :: ::: :::: : : :: :: ::: :::: : : :: :: ::: :::: : : :: :: : : :: :: :: :

THE PERSEIDS

:: :: :::: :: :: :::initiation:: :: :: :: ::: : ::: :virtualrealityrequest:: :: :: ::: ::: :: :: :: :: sequence:
:: :: ::1: :: ::: :00: ::: :: :: :1: :: :: :: : : : :: : : :: :: :[de]colonialreservations: :: :: :: :: ::: ::: :::
:::initiatingprojectionsequence: ::VR: :::request:::: :10011:: ::::apocalypseinitiated: :: :: ::

the mowers idle
in a field of yellowing canola
a soon-to-be
deep-fried kentucky thigh
in the mi-ki-nak convenience store

ill say my name in numbers
to forgo the twelve percent tax
on a few litres of gas
take home two-days-past-expired
bologna & macaroni
my kokum is hungry

going home –
a custard-kernelled sky,
peel into soot, into night;
& burning in the light
of a blood-orange supermoon
is the black-beaded eye
of a cyberbiorez dog
glistening

i pass him on the back road
dust clouds become his mane
as he fuses with the moon –
light tendrils illuminated
by my headlights:
a robonemean lion in the ditch

this is the single most dangerous object
known to humanity

"he can be this too,"
ill say
still seeing the eye
refracting in the turn signal,
"i could be that too"

WHAT I LEARNED IN PRE-CAL MATH

:: :: :::: :: :: :::initiation:: :: :: :: ::: : ::: :virtualrealityrequest:: :: :: ::: ::: :: :: :: :: sequence: :: :: ::1: :: ::: :00: ::: :: :: :1: :: ::: :: :: memoryextraction: :: :: :: :: ::painkillerrequest: ::: ::: :::initiatingwpgsequence: ::VR: :::request:::: :10011:: ::::dinnerscene: :: :: :: ::: :: :: :: ::: : :

we play this game
when we drink:
never have i ever
hyper-truth-or-dare
where we talk about
who-fucked-who
& when our latest bowel movement was

i look at her
in between bouts of jameson
& we know
to lock the trauma in a story
make them laugh
& theyll forget
wont ask if youre only being paranoid again
for conjuring your own debilitators
an exclusive sadomasochism best saved for
any non-white-hetero-person
to win the game, simply
screen a memory like a movie
filter it to filth
through adaptation
appropriation, cannibalization
homage & good intention:
tonight ill be a pretty woman
who dreams of beverly hills
& roommates named (first-aid) kit
tell myself: i can be a femme-boy fatal/e
instead i shop in portage place
urban ecko stitches
tv dinners in a yellow bag
thats giant tiger realness;

see my fist[questionmark]
its a matryoshka
middle, ring, index
my fingers can be mirrors

hereIamhereIamhereIam

never have i ever:
been downhill skiing
eaten cheese
had subway guacamole
– & drink

sigh a sigh of relief
vault the stories i was ready to make-believe
isnt a house party a confessional booth[questionmark]
smile at her across the room
my surrogate wife
realize i didnt have to tell them
about my first time having sex with a man
in a laundry room
atop my kokums nightgowns
when i dragged a mattress
to cover the door
hide us like mice
so we could fuck right proper
i thought:
ill be johnny rapid you be jake bass
fa:: :: :: ::lcon:: : :: :: ::video: :: :: :::: :downloadingpleasuresoftware: :: :: :: :::: :: : :: ::: : :: :
:: :: : : ::reconciled:: ::: ::vi:::::deo::::::::in::::stallation:::: ::com: :: ::: :: plete[me] :: : :: ::: :
instead we just jacked each other off
twisting our arms around a bottle of tide
& a crystal skull of vodka
: :: ::: ::: :::: :: ::: :[IN]digi[T]izingshake[spear]e: :: :: :: :: :: :: :: :: : :: ::: : :: : :: :: : :: :: :: : ::
to be or not to be: am i gay is the question[questionmark]
were just trades trading sex
do two negatives make a positive[questionmark]
never had to tell them about the time
i went home with a guy
after a greg ayres rave
hunchbacked in a delta hotel
neck splayed like an open wound
cock lacerates my throat
my larynx is a pinball machine
have a go at it, wont you[questionmark]
token for a play;
never had to tell them about the time
i was removed from the stage
of fame because i wouldnt take off my shirt
& the boy in green with reptilian eyes
simply let them push me off
if we came together
shouldnt we stay together

& why am i consoling you[questionmark]
never had to tell them about the time
when i let a man wrap himself
around me like an oyster
because i knew the boy i loved
couldnt love me as i am
& wandered downtown portage
at three a.m. knocking on the door
of my hosts apartment complex
my feet a blistered, bleeding mess
in a cowboy-toed spring shoe
the long walk of the 2S oji-cree
maybe im mercutio –
& relocation is my tybalt
but in this play the plague is mine
i still belong to no ones home;
never had to tell them about the time
i went home with a boy named josh
who i blew on my best friends couch
as her boxer-puppy watched
made him show me his drivers licence
to prove i wasnt just fucking myself
now i feel like a conservative pm
heres my quantum bloodline;
when i went home with a couple from new zealand
who grabbed my ass
& slid their fingers
between the buttons on my crotch
bought a box of condoms
& a big-bite at sev
cried on the curb at seven a.m.;
when i woke up in the bed
of a forty-year-old man
who slept atop my blazer
an imprint of his fingerprint
darkening on my forearm
goose-egg throbbing on the crown
this is my pseudo-scalp
thigh muscles overstretched
burning fibres in my hamstrings
taking forty dollars from his wallet
meander my way
down broadway in february
misrecognized at the marlborough
im just another drunken ndn
destined for the red
HEREiAMHEREiAMHEREiAM

after the game
when our heads are dazed
synapses lapsing with memory
funny how we remember so much
when were on the cusp of inebriation
we fall asleep together
holding one another
as real lovers are supposed to do
her thinking of another man
me too, i say, me too
in a bed spackled with peanuts
from a chocolate-covered drumstick
& ketchup from a big mac
breath condensing on the nose
or maybe thats just the booze
sweating from our skin[questionmark]
lips doing as hands do
saliva hot with exposé:
"if someone fucked us
while we were blacked out –
is that really making love[questionmark]"
but theres no fingers left to hold up
no vodka left in our drink
the breath we breathe
is a violent scream
these delights have bitter ends
best to laugh it off they say
got to keep that doctor away
& thats the real game, annit[questionmark]

i say good night
you know i love you, right[questionmark]
pretend im: :: :: ::: :: rome: :: :o
shes juliet –
smooth her roughness with a kunik
cusp my palm into hers
thats how holy rez-kids kiss
& we feel normal here, like this
ask myself:
am i really a thief[questionmark]
(& whore you[questionmark])
dont tell them
that shakespeare too stole ideas
were just refractions of reflections
here im just a fractal of the indigenous curve
& this still isnt a social phenomenon
this is simple geometry, really

APRIL 5: PASS[HANG]OVER

: ::: :: :: :: :: :initiating: : :: : : : :VR: : :: :request: : :: : : :sequence: :::: :: : :: : :
:teenagemasturbation: : : :channel:showcase: :::: ::: ::: scene: :: ::::installationcomplete: :: :: :: : ::

when i was a boy
i (dis)identified with roseanne barr –
i saw myself in darlene
& that excited me
terrifyingly

i used to skip school & stay up late on weekends
(when my parents worked at ikwe widdjiitiwin)
to watch queer as folk & kink on showcase
fantasize about brian kinney
dye my hair to look like justin taylor
catch brent everett & brent corrigan
in a brokeback bareback parody
(after the weather girl got naked)
feel guilty about jacking-off
to badboyton & mike18
(my first cybernetic boyfriends)
i was making mirrors out of white queers
whereami|whereami|whereami|
i|I[questionmark]

my easter chocolates arent hidden anymore
why bother when a hershey jesus
with wonky eyes will cost $2.99 tomorrow[questionmark]
if anything i want to resurrect
the toughest ndn in the world
ask him, "whats it like to be a swiss army knife
& have hardcore anal sex[questionmark]"
maybe even ask him, "hey cuzzin
can you teach me how to be
a beautiful brown boy in love[questionmark]"

instead i dance in pool halls to rihanna
"bitch better have my money"
wait for the sharks to get horny
get them off for another beer
reassure them that everyones a little gay
honey-boo-boo even told me so
channel apu to exoticize myself
be a jack-of[F]-all-ndns
"thank you, come again"
tell him, "hey bo'
this is treaty 1 territory
so you may as well treat yourself too"

THE FA—[TED] QUEENE, AN IPIC P.M.

A Gentle Knight was pricking on the plaine,
Ycladd in mightie armes & siluer shielde
Where1n: ::: :old::dints : : of d::ee::p::e:::w::0u:n:d: ::s:d1d:r: : :: e: ::m: :: :: a: :: :i: :::
:n:e: :: : :: :: : : :: :: :: :: ::: :::: : ::: :: ::: :::[instealling software]:: :: :: :::: : :: :: :::: : : ::
:press: :: :::: ::x: :: ::: :: :: :: :::: : :: ::[instealling. . .] : :: :: :: : ::[instealling. . .]: :: :: :::: :: ::: :
[insteallation complete]: :: :: :: :::::: ::::[runningpro(1,0)zoaprogram]: :::: ::: : ::: :: ::
:[target]: ::: ::: : :::[redcrosseknight]: :: :::: :: ::::: :: ::: :: :: :: : :[indigenizationcomplete]:

peyak[period]

1 am the red crosse knight
patr0n of true hol1nesse
thank you: :: spenser: :::
for m0u1ng me to westerne sh[or]e
whom to auenge, you ask[questionmark]
una had from far compeld
i am here to reuenge
slay dragons in monks robes sterne
reuiue pregnant-medusa-natives
you sterilized to teach yourself
what it means to be a holy man
in caues of err by which you [me]an
in arabie, ynde, indo-indian, orientall america
my continent is the house of holiness
you may not enter, it is not accessible
i am soureigne here, hight reuerence
spacious courts with dens of errour
meant to trap settlers like you
"be well aware," your white duessa beckons
this is no place for liuing men
& all settlers are zombie imperialists
nikâwiys stomach
whom you, red crosse, slayed
was full of bookes & papers
sewed onto her belly
from boarding schools & priests pens
religious zealots poison bile evangelical propaganda
i am her child
the perill of this place
this is the wandring wood
iktomi brought you to me
to you: i am a monster vile
& i dont care if god does hate
i am zoa
halfe like a man the other halfe
did womans shape retaine

i am the things that nightmares are made of
when you dream of guilt
youll see me
riddled in wildernesse wetdreams of shame
i am the indigenous bogeyman
you should fear me
i am the most lothsom, filthie, foule
& full of vile disdaine
did you not see me in jekyll & at oka[questionmark]
in the bones of chief theresa spence
you cannot kill me, red crosse
i haue timely pride aboue the ndn vale
dualistic duessa dingy dugouts
take a step, snare in my snaps
euery breath you make to read these words
i [half]breed ten thousand
kindes of creatures, partly male
& partly female of my fruitfull seede
do you feel me around your loin
i will sterilize you as you did nikâwiy
my huge traine wounds around your waist
you striue in vaine
as i squeeze your organs, pained
god helpe the man so wrapt
in indigenous errours endlesse traine
no god here, this is native country
there is only nikâwiy & i
whom youve tried to rape & kill
so unto you i pronounce ~~death~~pîmâcisiwin
& squash you in my hands;
while i may be encombred sore
the native in me you could not hurt at all

nîso[period]

to the princesse of holinesse, faire
una, soon to be laissez-fair[i]e queene:
run, little lamb, run
for the woods are mine
dark & deep
in ndn country i am soureigne;
i poured forth out of my hellish sinke
my fruitfull cured spawne of serpents small
red as erred inke, which swarm about her legs
& infect for she is fearfull more of shame
than of an all-too-easy death;
my scattered brood to who i am parent deare
down her party rudely & all fall to the ground

groning full of deadly guilt, troubled with feare,
faire una, whom my children gath[red] themselues
about her body round
knockt her brest, cried to repent
& i, with my indigenous legion, spawn of zoa
dragged her to her chappell edifyde
deepe in the forests side
unleashed unto her my nehiyaw daughters
fidelia, sperenza & charissa
or as i call them:
metoni ka peyakohetohk, pakoseyimowin & ka nahâwehk
who pull from the ground
a mound of earth
the sacred booke, with bloud ywrit
that none could read, except peyakohetohk
who disclosed euery whit
that weaker wit of man could neuer reach
of manitou, of grace, of justice, of free will
peyakohetohk, parting the flouds in tway
could eke huge mountaines from their native seat
& unto the faire una she did pierce
the word repeat the wounds of our dear mother
unto the tongue of the princess holiness
red crosses dearest una did behold
disdaining life, desiring leaue to die
she found her selfe assayld with great perplexitie;
next, pakoseyimowin, coming to that
soule-diseased princess
did apply reliefe of leaues & mawka root
which had passing priefe
but yet the cause & root of all this ill
inward corruption, outward colonization
not purg'd nor heal'd, behind remain'd still
in ashes & sackcloth did pakoseyimowin put una in
daintie corse, proud humors to abate
she made una pray both earely & eke late:
& euer as superfluous flesh did rot
brought forth the zombie from her flesh-made-cot
& plucked it out with pincers fyrie whott
that soone in her was lefte no one corrupted iott;
last, ka nahâwehk, with a vined whip,
pricked with sharp spines at the base of its leaues,
was wont her once to discipline euery day:
that sharpe remorse her heart did pricke & nip,
the drops of bloud thence like a well did play;
& sad repentance used to embay
her body euen whiter
in salt water smarting sore

the filthy blots of history to wash away
the woman that was sentenced to death
but earst lay at deathes dore;
faire una, in her torment, which was so great
that she, like a lion, did cry & roar
una, whom my children did rend flesh & sinews eat
cleansed the wretched of the earth
granted death unto the power in her whiteness
left her a newborn babe, now reconciled
hauing killed the white child in the ndn
did tell unto her: "the choice now is yours
whether you liue or die[period]"

i climbed the hill of contemplation
snared the priests who threw their holy writs
which they aimed at my greatness
& planted the head of sir george
high atop its peak
shouted into the distances
in which the citie of the great king sat
in haughty view steaming smoke
feeling my auenging wrath to clemencie incline
& towards the empire i cried:
"we haue our strength recur'd from fraile infirmitis
with bloudy letters by the hand of Manitou
& washed my hands from guilt of bloudy field
that i moue unto your great city
with little remorse & absolutely no pity
for now are we come unto my native soyle
this place, where all your perils dwell
here i haunte you feend, here does
colonialism dayly spoyle;
to all moniyaw, be wary
for i haue decided, against your many sins
to take action against all you haue done"
& in the distance was heard
the rallying cry of euery nehiyaw
who emerged from their caues of err,
satyrs, faeries, cyborg niizh-manitoag imperialists,
all rose their fists into the air
& all, in unison, proclaimed:
"death to the red crosse,
death to their vaults
death to their inherited, neo-colonizing faults"
& euery nehiyaw in earshot agreed
to raise the dragon & burn
their wâpiskâw cities to the ground

SLAY BELLS REIGN IN SUBURBIA

eb: : :: bb: ::in::::ezzz::::er::::scr:o:0:ge:: :: :: :downloadingdickenssoftware: :: : :: :: :: :: ::
:: :::::: :: : :: : ::: : :: : :: : : : : :: ::installationcomplete: :: :: : ::: :: :: :::::: : :: :: ::: :: :: :::: : : :
: : no space
of re – grit[questionmark]: :: ::can u make amen – d: :: :: ::s[questionmark]
for
o:n:epluso:n:e:o:n:epluso:n:e:o:n:epluso:n:e:o:n:epluso:n:e:o:n:epluso:n:e:o:n:epluso:n:e:
lifes opportunity mis[used][taken][
can your settler guilt amend that[questionmark]
hereiamscroogescrewingyou: :: :: :: ::: :::::: : : ::: :: :: :: : :: : : :: :::
feel my ghosts digging in your bone
i may be a bit of beef cowhide tanhide leather fetish
a pound of lard & flour
ratio reckoning on the long walk of the navajo – ahohohoho
theres a fraction of the refracted fracking system here on the table
a pound of oil for you, a pound of flesh for me
more gravy than grave about me, whoever i am[imscrooge
whoreu[questionmark]]

my body has dreams of bruised|r i p p e dflesh
i fucking hate new england
wo[m]vo[an]ka tells me she was raped by ten men
i said, im sick of dreaming
they scare me mommy
she says: theyre yours, keep them there, theyre delightful little things – dreams
are a far superior requiem than the precarity of our day-to-day t
i ask: whos "they"[questionmark] i
she says: go to bed, my son, its trad – its christ – m
ition mas[period] e

youarefetteredtellmewhy[questionmark]
isityourguiltthatmakesyouso –
do you tremble in your sheets like a wannabe ghost dreaming of christmas since past
isityourguiltthatmakesyouso –
do you drown yourself in remembrance knowing full well you too-too-took my girls life
wearthechainsyouforgedinlife –
links linked by history yard by yard across the plateau the heavy weight of rousseau & cartier & old king henry & elizabeth on the twenty beheaded marys who spill blood like red women on the highway of tears
you are f-e-t-t-e-r-e-d:here:y-o-u:are
this is tradition right[questionmark]
let me subject you to mine:
squeeze into the uterus, pouch your testicles into your gooch, wear a skirt|skit to enter the

circle, change your name, cut your hair, watch your own brothers kill the parts of you that
let you love, that tell you youre niizh manitoag & beautiful & wonderful & loved
kill all of that & mope around into a ball of ooze to be kicked around by settlers &
traditionalists alike, infect yourself with disease & sorrow – this is the ghost dance
        wovoka, iktomi, nanabozho – all are hungry for a settlers soul
        this is for the people who love you [oldelizabethisasdeadasadoornailnow]

i am the ghost of natives past;
 the ghost of colonialism present;
  the ghost of settlers to come
 i live past|present|future
        the spirits of all three strive within me
        learn the lessons they have to teach
        & run afeard in the wake of the trc
here i am
        you have never seen the likes of me before
                                this is for y – o – u
                                 ebenezer scrooge
                                                bah humbug to you too

i regard your apology as the deadest piece of ironmongery in this new trade
        the wisdom of my ancestors is in this extended simile
                touch it, i dare you – this countrys done for
words from your fathers cling to me like muck::rake
your boys are ignorance & your girls are want
beware them both if you want me
moreso, settler scrooge,
fear me:
rage&hunger&doom
are furrowed in the braids
that you so covet
& i raise my brows to you

ps marleywasdead:tobeginwith –

RE(Z)ERVING PARADISE

a p.m. for t.c.

: :: : :: :: : : :: :: :: :: ::: :::: : ::: :: ::: :::[instealling miltonsoftware]:: :: :: :::: : :: :: :::: : : ::
:press: :: :::: ::x: :: ::: :: :: :: :::: : :: ::[instealling. . .] : :: :: :: : ::[instealling. . .]: :: :: :::: :: ::: :
[insteallation complete]: :: :: :: :::::: ::::[runningpro(1,0)zoaprogram]: :::: ::: : ::: :: ::
:[target]: ::: ::: : :::[re|decolonizing]: :: :::: :: ::::: :: ::: :: :: :: : :[indigenizationcomplete]:

when i look at my aunt
take laboured breaths in a paralyzed body
thats comatose|comingapart at the seams
i think of john milton
i wonder what losing paradise means
for a thirty-nine-year-old ndn mother of six[questionmark]
i wonder if shes making a heaven of hell
for every moment her eyes refuse to open
i wonder if she still feels the sting of gravel
on her face from when she paralyzed herself
on the back roads of the reservation
i wonder what it must be like to not be able to respond
to your own mother asking: “where have you gone[questionmark]”

i touch her earlobe
wonder if she lives there now[questionmark]
when we have no body
we make the weirdest of homes
we have lived in smaller places
we have lived in torture chambers
her body twitches when i touch her face
we are furnished in beauty
& finished in breath –
i lipsync to a wannabe-ndn asking:
where are ü now[questionmark]

the name on the screen says teri
i write a post-it note & stick it over
theres two “rs” in your name, shes not fucking teriyaki;
when i look at her now i see edvard munch
his scream has nothing on her face
her bottom jaw is slightly extended beyond her upper
lips cracked – drying in the icu
her tongue protrudes when she tries to smile
which is few & far between;

her knuckles – ive never noticed her knuckles before
never seen how much richer

the brownness of her skin is on her knuckles
i wonder why & think of stories – stories of rez fights
& her long black hair whipping around
on the monkey bars & on the merry-go-round
her tongue constantly convulses in her mouth

– her eyes strain to open
i hear my mom saying, "dont cry, my girl"
my aunts face is a perpetual scream
i look at it from her left side
the highs&lows of her face
the bump of her chin & nose
the trident of her cupids bow
the furrow of her brow
& a few single strands of grey hair
tucked behind her ear
damp with sweat from a fever that wont break;

i think: what the fuck am i doing writing a poem
while my aunt is dying in front of my eyes[questionmark]

i notice i keep from crying by telling her jokes
i tell her: "now that you have grey hair
meryl streep has nothing on you, auntie"
tell her: "hey do you remember the time
you pretended to be my mom & called in sick
for me at school so i didnt have to go to swimming classes[questionmark]"
tell her: "youre waking up, right[questionmark]
you owe me a bingo night & your daughter wants to play rock band with you"
tell her: "your sons in my bedroom building a telescope of lego
so that he can watch you fall asleep every night"
i dont want to tell her its because i think he knows
what we know
& wants to build a contraption so that he can spy on you wherever you go
tell her: "im glad the last time we spoke
i said i loved you, but im sorry i had to be drunk to do it"

i stare at her ear to keep composed
while the women around me cry&cry&cry
& for some fucking reason i think of whitman
tell him: fuck you, you colonial fuck
the leaves of trees have really only taught me
how beautiful a show it is
to die&die&die
tell milton that he can fuck off too:
you cant make a heaven of hell
if the promise of heavens always been hellish to you;

tell munch he should go fuck himself as well
what does he know about horror –
since when do settlers know how to scream[questionmark]

i look at my aunts earlobe
see the hole where an earring used to sit
think about how many madonna songs these ears have listened to[questionmark]
i see a beauty mark in her ear canal
it winks at me, i swear
thats when i know
that native lives are precarious things
were never promised more than today
but there is beauty too, i think,
were more than the sum of our suffering cells
while my family cries
while my aunts face becomes the scream
i see another in her ear
a smiling woman with brown eyes
that winks & says: hereiamhereiam
& as i follow her into the cerebellum
i see: she hasnt made a heaven of hell
but rather, she said, “fuck this yankee doodle hospital
ive made a hell of your idyllic heaven
& called it decolonial loving”

CAN YOU BE MY FULLTIME DADDY: WHITE&GOLD[QUESTIONMARK]

: :: :: : : ::::: : : :: : : : :installingmusicsoftware: : :: :::: : : :: ::borntodierecordinstalled: :: : : :::: :: ::: :: :: convertingappropriationintoadaptation: : :: ::::: pleasewait: : ::::: :: :: : :: ::: :: : :deleteheaddress[questionmark]:: :: ::::: : :: :: Y: :: :: :: : : :: : ::::: installationcomplete: :::

i was in the winter of my life
& the men i met along the road
were my only summer
heating my thighs with hands
that were warm yet pinching;
at night i fall asleep with visions of myself
bleeding, dancing, singing:
"theres an ndn
chanting in the dead of night
& she says take your broken bones;
learn to write"
i cry with these dreams
how did williams, whitman & ginsberg
see themselves as beautiful things?
twenty years down the line
im still banking on the promise of an ndn giver;
these memories of my family
are the only things that sustain me
even if i have to conjure them
as ghosts in the machine
dancing puppets on the prairie
solicit me, solace me
give me approximation proxy
adopted ancestral adaptations:
heres a photo of me saying
i wish i had said goodbye when you died
i wish the reservation wouldnt deny
cant i be an ndn too?
why is my ethnicity always lacking proof?
are two brown boys in love not injun enough?
when i say ~~(nikâwiy)~~ mother in cree
it still tastes like a dirty thing –
& i see nôhkum
blooming in saskatoon
the land of rape & honey
shes the breath of babies now
i huff her scent every morning;
i see my cousins
burning in a fire
arms akimbo, fingers askew

nailbeds embedded in riverbeds
the deep flow of our dna
in the river red;
i see the cancers in my father
the diabetes in my mother
how much time do we really have?
can iktomi trick you into lying
here in these memory beds
that snatch like spider silk
i caught you, ill hold you
but i know youll never be mine
kisâkihitin, kisâkihitin –
these are the only real happy times
i have left;
i was a storyteller
& not a very popular one
i once had dreams of becoming a beautiful poet
but upon an unfortunate present
saw those dreams dashed, divided
peppered & burnt in the sky
hazing the sun
with words, with stories
with tricksters howling in pain;
here are my people

moulding in the gutters of a psa
canadian heritage moments
i wish over & over
to be these things
be everything for everyone
but im just one man
one sad red poofter
brazen & broken
moulting in july;
i dont really mind
because i was born knowing
that it takes getting everything you ever wanted
& then losing it to know
what liberalism truly feels like;
& i cry into the night
singing with my ancestors
proud & loud
"if we cannot be free
let us die
what is life to a caged bird
threatened by death on all sides?"
& when the people i used to know

find out what i have been doing
how ive identified
they ask me why –
why do you play ndn now?
dont you still taste ddt
in your mouth when you say these words to me?
but theres no use in talking to people who have a home
they have no idea what its like to seek your kind
for safety in numbers
for home to be wherever you lay your head
for relocation to be a homestead;
& when i found them on a back road
we decided we had nothing left to lose
nothing to gain, nothing we desired anymore
except to make our lives heard
to be beautiful once more;
i was always an unusual boy
my mother told me i had a tricksters soul
no moral compass pointing north
no fixed personality, gender
just an inner indecisiveness that was as wide
as wavering as smouldering sweetgrass
on the horizon, blind;
& if you say you didnt plan for it to turn out this way –
youd be lying
because i was born to be the other man
who belonged to no one, who belongs to everyone
who had nothing & wanted everything
with a cigarette burn for every experience
& an obsession, as they call it, with freedom
that terrifies me to the point
that i can only hum it in a poem
that pushes me to a nomadic point of madness
a past they all want to see
im an ndn –
that both dazzles & dizzies me;
so i suppose i find it hard to find the time to live
when i so often want to be left alone
im afraid of love, that smothering embrace
the lingering danger of benevolence
you always ask me to taste
for if i let you
youll love me to death
suffocate me with your suffix
your grammar squanders
it squishes
your papers cut me

& hugs strangle, gently
the hanging indent of a goodwill iou
great "X" on the signature line
so i just ride
to the west
looking for the country kanata used to be
i ride
i ride
i ride
just hoping to
c a t c h

m
y b
r
e

a

t

h –

E/ESPYWITHMYLITTLE(I)

: :: ::: :: : : : :installingchildhoodsoftware: :wherethehelliswaldoapplicationinstalled: :: :
::deletecloakingsoftware[questionmark]: : :: :::Y:::pleasewait: : ::::: :: :: : :: ::: :: : ::: ::::::::
:: Y: :: :: :: : : :: : ::::: installationcomplete: :::: :: :: ::: :: :: :: :: : :: : : :: : :: : : : ::: : :: : : ::: ::

there is a guilt
that pulls
feel wrong
for a few brief seconds
shame being an affront
on canadian character
not on the pain
that throbs in the bone
my confession has no merit
in health – it is always an attack;
when you tell me, “not everything
is about race” i say, “yeah
but i woke up & lived
as a poc today”
every word i breathe life into
is a vessel, a weapon
waking up alive
makes me a politic –
sometimes
i only want to be heard
& not called a killjoy
or a naysayer
can i just be,
too[questionmark]

why is my p[>>] (ai) [<<]n the thing to
u
all i am
n
is organ –
izer, spirit-stick for
all-inclusive-poca(honest[questionmark])-retreats
d
peacepipe for post-neo-spiritualists
practising down(ward)-dog-tibetan-yoga
tantric-doggy-anal-positioning
o[questionmark]
(which ndn am i[questionmark])
contemplating white buffalo
ethnographic shanty (getaway)
on drill-zone-prairie-reservations
if i am not the cutified war chief
smoking ayahuasca

trading land for pogs
& contemplating crying
over highway litter

if not those things
iamthepoliticiamwrongiamshameiamiamiamshameiamhereiamiamiamiamshameiamiami:
:a:m:i:a:m:i:a:m:i:a:m:i:a:m:i:a:m:i:a:m:i:a:m:i:a:m:i:a:m:i:a:m:i:a:m:i:a:h:e:r:e:i:a:m:i:a:m:i:a:
m:i:a:m:i:a:m:i:a:m:i:a:m:i:a:m:i:a:m:i:a:h:e:r:e:i:a:m:i:a:m:i:a:m:i:a:m:i:a:m:i:a:m:i:a:m:i:a:m:i:a:m:
i:a:m:i:a:m:i:a:m:i:a:m:i:a:m:i:a:m:i:a:m:i:a:m:i:a:m:i:a:m:i:a:m:i:a:m:i:a:m:i:a:m:a:m:i:a:m:i:a:m:i:a:m:i:a:
m:i:a:m:i:a:m:h:e:r:e:a:m:i:a:m:i:a:m:i:a:m:i:a:m:i:a:m:i:a:m:i:a:m:i:a:m:i:a:m:i:a:m:i:h:e:r:e:i:a:m:i:a:
iloopthesewordsinmyheaduntiltheylosetheirmeaninguntil**IAM**beginstoquestion
itself**AMI**untilthewordbreaksapart&thenounbecomesthreelettersjitteringaboutlike
dislocatedmagnets**IAM**becomes**AMI**whichbecomes**A-M-I**whenigooglewhatmeans
AMIiamtoldthatinjapanese**AMI**meanslove&infrench**AMI**meansfriend&inhebrew**AMI**m
eansmypeoplebuttome**AMI**meansnoneofthosethingswhenisayspeakthislanguagemytongu
eburnsandmymouthstilltastesofddtwhenisaythesewordsallifeelisguiltyspitmynameoutofyo
urmouth&dontyoufuckingtellmehowtofeelitypeintogooglebuticantpress[**ENTER**]thatmak
esitrealmakesmevisibleandthosekeystheywanttoscalpmeamistillthepoliticmy[**DEL**]keyis
mysaviourglowinginitswhitehotlightwhenilookreallycloseiseemyfingerprintgreased
ontothekeythereiam&thatfeelsgoodbestto**[DEL]**idontwanttofeelguiltyagainmaybeiam[que
stionmark]
idontknowidontknowidontknowidontknowidontknowidontknowidontknowallthatremainsisthis:
s

i

l

e

n

c

e that rings in my
(h)ear(iam)

REFLECTIONS ON LITTLE [BULLHEAD]

:: :: :::: :: :: :::initiation:: :: :: :: ::: : ::: :virtualrealityrequest:: :: :: ::: ::: :: :: :: :: sequence: ::
:: ::1: :: ::: 0: ::: :: :: :1: :: :: :: : : : :: : : :: :: :[de]coloniallibraries: :: ::derridaarchivefound:
:: :::rewrite[questionmark] ::: :::Y:: :::initiatinglocatingsequence: ::VR: :::request:::: : :: :::
::10011:: ::::here1am: :: :: :: :: :: : winnipegpubliclibrary:: :: : :: ::: :::::: :: :: :: ::: ::: : :::: :

"dublin dan"
was a fine, fine man –
& i wonder how much he
would pay me for a photo of
my cock[questionmark]
i found dans name in a book
titled *man –*
itoba as I saw it from 1869
to date
along with a written note
& a photo pasted over the cover
"do you know him[questionmark]"
its dated christ –
mas 1909:
"i wish you to live a hundred years
& i hope to live a hundred years
less a day
for i have no wish to live
when my old friend has passed away"
charles james
& if you curtail the "o" in "old," curs –
ive style, it almost looks like "red"
"my red friend has passed away"
now thats a story i can believe

i wonder if they were lovers[questionmark]
this dan, this charles
which one was the top[questionmark]
which the bottom[questionmark]
which the christian[questionmark]
which the redskin[questionmark]
& 106 years later
at christmas, yet
i still get in fist fights
at the band office
because i wear my pants too tight
all i want is my handout
same as anybody else

in the book
there are pictures
of old dead white men
who adorn their names
with hyphenated honours
& split proper nouns to fill the page
(why do hyphens work for them[questionmark]):
honourablesenatorturnerlieutenantgovernorarchibald&evenhisgracearchbishop
l y n c h
i have trouble telling them apart
the only significant difference
is the mutton chops
that frisk their faces
– & i like that word, mutton
(but im not supposed to want) –

there are photos of cpr,
a little school
erect on the prairie
an ox plowing the field
& kanji written in pencil on the page
questioning: what means constituency[questionmark]
little hearts & exclamation marks deco
"natives objected to his wearing purple"
i write back: AMI
but it doesnt feel right for a book like this
i need to take out the M,
AI means love

i flip to a photo of
major general cameron:
"rielwasadangerouscrank**h**alflunaticitwasnotalwaysth**e**samep**r**iestbutallspok**e**alongpac**i**ficl
ines**a**llaytheturbulenceinthe**m**indsofthe**h**alfbr**e**edsitmustbe**r**ememb**e**redthatthenat**i**veswere
beinginstructedbytheirownspiritu**a**ladvisersandwouldnaturallybeinsy**m**pathywit**h**th**e**mthe**r**
ewasonepr**i**est**a**french**m**anandw**h**il**e**iamnotawa**r**eofhisp**e**rsonalsympathyw**i**ththeuprisingof
then**a**tivesduringthei**m**prisonmenti**h**av**e**thoughthisviews**r**ath**e**rradical"
– my mothers maiden name is cameron
& i think back to my french grandfather, rene
who left me a roll of film
after he died –
it was the first time i met that part
of my f a m i l y
"well catch up, well talk, we will, i pro –"
white wishes, white lies
a minor benign falsehood

(benign being a gentle thing
that diseases, that kills)
twenty dollars & gas
station lollipops
wouldnt feed a rez dog
never mind a grandchild –
                i give him mutton chops too

& sorry cameron
106 years later
i have not yet been allayed
& *that* must be remembered

i close the book
put it back on the shelf
notice the harsh black tape
that still holds it together
the book is staining daily
it eats itself, simply
its foxing
silly little thing
maybe in a hundred years more
youll finally disappear

& thats the real trick
aint it[questionmark]
ahahahahahahahahahahahahahahahahahahahahahahahahahahahahahahahahahahahahahahahaha
ahahahahahahahahahahahahahahahahahahahahahahahahahahahahahahahahahahahahahahahaha
ahahahahahahahahahahahahahahahahahahahahahahahahahahahahahahahahahahahahahahahaha
ahahahahahahahahahahahahahahahahahahahahahahahahahahahahahahahahahahahahahahahaha
ahahahahahahahahahahahahahahahahahahahahahahahahahahahahahahahahahahahahahahahaha
ahahahahahahahahahahahahahahahahahahahahahahahahahahahahahahahahahahahahahahahaha
ahahahahahahahahahahahahahahahahahahahahahahahahahahahahahahahahahahahahahahahaha
ahahahahahahahahahahahahahahahahahahahahahahahahahahahahahahahahahahahahahahahaha
ahahahahahahahahahahahahahahahahahahahahahahahahahahahahahahahahahahahahahahahaha
ahahahahahahahahahahahahahahahahahahahahahahahahahahahahahahahahahahahahahahahaha
ahahahahahahahahahahahahahahahahahahahahahahahahahahahahahahahahahahahahahahahaha
ahahahahahahahahahahahahahahahahahahahahahahahahahahahahahahahahahahahahahahahaha
ahahahahahahahahahahahahahahahahahahahahahahahahahahahahahahahahahahahahahahahaha
ahahahahahahahahahahahahahahahahahahahahahahahahahahahahahahahahahahahahahahahaha
ahahahahahahahahahahahahahahahahahahahahahahahahahahahahahahahahahahahahahahahaha
ahahahahahahahahahahahahahahahahahahahahahahahahahahahahahahahahahahahahahahahaha
ahahahahahahahahahahahahahahahahahahahahahahahahahahahahahahahahahahahahahahahaha
ahahahahahahahahahahahahahahahahahahahahahahahahahahahahahahahahahahahahahahahaha
ahahahahahahahahahahahahahahahahahahahahahahahahahahahahahahahahahahahahahahahaha
!

"D" PAIRS WELL WITH VOWELS

:: :: :::: :: :: :::initiation:: :: :: :: ::: : ::: :virtualrealityrequest:: :: :: ::: ::: :: :: :: :: sequence: ::
:: ::1: :: ::: :0: ::: :: :: :1: :: :: :: : : : :: : : :: :: :[de]colonialtimetravel: :: :: :: :: ::: ::: ::: :: : ::
:: :::initiatingjumpersequence: ::VR: :::request:::: :10101:: ::::queertime: ::ndntime :: :: ::

when my orthodontist
asks my age
i want to tell him:
eighteen, maybe, nineteen
i round it up to twenty
& add a year
make my *s e l f* [fit]
"im twenty-five"
(or was it twenty-six[questionmark])
i believe
as much as he does
when he nods & says,
"mmhmm"
i say, "hmm"
share my life through
onomatopoeic static –
memory is such a fickle thing:
i am a man of ash
(& isnt that just funny[questionmark])

when my friends ask why
i lie about my age
i tell them, "its a queer thing"
i dont tell them that i think their cult –
ure(s) stole twenty years from me:
twenty to come out
one to (un)learn
one to (re)learn
& four to wander around lost&neverfound
i guess its an ndn thing too
(hereiam on a milk carton priced at $19.99)
in supermarkets, alleyways
on (res)ervations, (res)identical streets
this is my (res)identity: xxix
babygay, babyboy, ndninthecloset
im still a child through&through
– instead i just tell them i
fancy wilde men, wild things
spend too much time in mirrors
staring at jekyll, assessing my hyde

i hate my body because i structured queerness
around the plot line of regina george
& instead of sears
i shop for clothes at hbc

i give my body up
its ruined anyways –
from transfigurations
written on my skin
i am not the author of my being –
give myself like a winter donation
to siloam missions down princess avenues
this is jan, mb
(but isnt that what they want[questionmark])
a coat of flesh to line the hoods
of a canadian-goose exped(ition) parka
id rather you tailor it with a military stitch
& call it what it really is: neo-redcoat

cant i just be a body that loves[questionmark]
why do i have to be a thing[questionmark]
i exist in the bone
& nothing really matters

plath once said that like a cat
she has nine-times to die
me too! this is number four
the kill-site is spread wide;
ill spend a few lives more
in the matter of this minute

like plath i too enjoy a hot bath
but it is no cure-all
far too often i observe my skin
& when it loosens in the heat
i am happy that it changes:
it takes a dash of white to pinken red –
but my nipples are still darker than my chest
& my hairs are a telling cue
when i *have* hair it is dark & curly
a hot bath never did too much
im still just a "dirty indian":
the miracle of skin was in its elasticity
not only for the birth of children
but for wrapping around the old pain
without burst or fear of cyst
i have to make peace

with my|self
every evening
wrapped in my duvet
shifting through reruns of rpdr
in this too-too big house
explore by hand
my abdo/men
feel for the bone
& think: “this is okay
this will do”

a second makes for a torturing device
& patience is a killing tool

while i wait, w a i t , w a i   t
for everything to click
& am forced to reanimate
re/member hashed memories –
i turn myself to ash;
my minds a barren wasteland
deco/ed with triggers
ashmen in the bare
waiting for a soft wind
(chinook as they say) to blow
me all away
it really is that fucking simple
pull this trigger
see what happens

its three a.m.
i suppose “technically”
its another day
& im still the same
i guess ill just have to wait another
day

a [n o t (h e r)]

d
a
y

a

n

o

t

h

e

r

d

a

y

d

a

y

d

a

y

I CAN BE A DREAM GIRL TOO

:: :: :::: :: :: :::initiation:: :: :: :: ::: : ::: :virtualrealityrequest:: :: :: ::: ::: :: :: :: :: sequence: ::
:: ::1: :: ::: :00: ::: :: :: :1: :: :: :: : : : : :: : : :: :: :queerkinshipsequence: :: :: :: :: ::: ::: ::: : :: ::
::::initiatingdragsequence: ::VR: :::request:::: :10011:: :::transformationscene: :: :: :: :: : ::

rupaul once said that
"there is nothing more sad than the tears of a drag queen"
when trixie mattel told her story about her father
i cried along with her
i could hear the sirens, the yelling
the pots&pans, shattering budweiser
i thought: me too, me too
these are the stories i have

a good memory is a dream
laced with some underlying pain
& the waking desire to (re)create
from the fragments of a few seconds
nowadays i forget which is real
which is dreamt[questionmark]
dreamscapes are scapegoats
so why stop boozing now[questionmark]
& it often feels like life or death
asking us to quit drinking
often it is –
i need a depressant to offset
the deep depression;
im feeling nostalgic here tonight
then again, so is every other ndn

i look through my fathers photo album
see nôhkums obituary
headline reads: "funeral is only chance for reunion:
indians have no fund to reunite adopted-out families"
i see my dad sitting on some steps
looking sullen, looking ndn
wonder if he knows the people that are coming
are benefactors of the sixties scoop
(european bene[dic]tion tastes a lot like kielbasa)
think: damn, he looks a lot like me
isthatmeisthatmeisthatme
find myself as a three-year-old tot
smiling, running towards the camera
a bright-pink neon windbreaker
wonder if anyones ever looked at their own photograph

& wanted to say:
"im sorry about all the mistakes i made"

i cant help but blame settlement
for the deaths within my family:
my three-year-old cousin
drinking hairspray thinking it is water
my kokum scraping his tonsils
with her fingers
theres toxin in there too
now he (rez)ides in the youth centre
(orange you glad i didnt say piper chapman[questionmark])
there are babies screaming for amoxicillin
oxymoronic fathers popping oxycontin
in a burning house that smells of frybread;
there are newborns named after fathers
whowerealcoholicswhohadsonswhowerealcoholics
the wheel has come full circle
funny theres no ndn named king lear;
there are starving children in the housing projects
who eat five-cent sour dinosaurs instead of apples
& are blamed for their own diabetes;
adoctoradayadoctoradayadoctoraday;
unpaid mothers who trade food stamps
for actual stamps in the moloch-machine
we call the baby factory
when child-tax day is the bane of walmarts workweek;
there are two toddlers crying for their mother
whos paralyzed herself on the peguis back roads
pontiac montana crunched into a snowball;
i cannot *not* want to hate
or hate my*self* for forgiving
parenthetical paradox: shamehateshame
im always [for]giving
wilfully forgetting
sorry nôhkum
its the way of the white:
forgive, forget, [for]go
or was it simply:
eat, pray & love[questionmark]

when rupaul announces her booster-project background
& sashays across a court with no nets
i live
(re)memory: myself playing horse with the housing kids
"you better werk[exclamationmark]"
i want to be a supermodel of the world
spread my legs for mac cosmetics

instead of ious on chatroulette
& dick pics on snapchat amateur hour
to top off this months rent
"you better werk," i repeat
"off that community service, maybe"

i used to fantasize about tiffany
draped in diamonds like holly golightly
(do you think they serve fried bologna for breakfast there[questionmark])
think about her last name
wonder if she knows thomas builds-the-fire[questionmark]
(yeah, ive never met him either
but ive been larry sole at house parties)
i sing "i think im alone now"
as the other kids craft longbows
out of willow branches
to match the welts on their forearms
call me during the latter half of their game
cast me as we'wha the berd[acḥe]
for that spackle of authenticity
that greasepaint cant afford
in their premier frontier fantasy
~~og~~[oh]lala they say

& i always agreed
to exchange my scalp for a lip-sync
in the wide expanse of little grand rapids
"there doesnt seem to be anyone around"
/endscene
ah, the irony
the verisimilitude of the cree milieu
two truths, one lie
i am the tonto ndnness
"you&you&you
youre going to love me"
& one of us is lying

its such an odd world
we have to live in
for the prefix-addiction liberalism harbours
post –
racial, sexual, colonial
why dont we ask what means
stress[questionmark]trauma[questionmark]resident[questionmark]
what does it mean to survive your father
who lost two sons in the latest rez-fire[questionmark]

why am i always adapting your words
from latin tongues & french theorists
ive mastered my masters language
ill need a tic tac after this poem

so i just cry when trixie mattel returns to rpdr
i too have been a trixie to my father
take her advice, know my worth & demand three times that
& when they ask, "whats my occupation[questionmark]"
ill reply, "settle, settle"
for once the joke is on you
~~feel like all is right in the world:~~
i have to stop myself
remember that my people are dying
during every metaphor in this poem
dying, dying,
go –

A[U] CLA[I]R THE L[OWN]E

when i sent him lilies for christmas
he asked, "is this really how you feel[questionmark]"
& i was ashamed
so i joked, saying, "sometimes i like me too"
"thats not what i meant," he said
& i sighed, yes, it is –
* * *
i do have a god-shaped hole in my heart
i told him that it comforts me
even though its heartbreaking as hell
i said, "sometimes you just need to realize
that youre wounded to know
youre lovely in there too"
told him, "you know, tupac shakur grew
roses in concrete
& at the end of the day
richard wagamese got sober & loved joshua
thats worth something, annit[questionmark]"
tell him that i feel so many things every day
that each hour traumatizes me in some small way
that when i get home & undress for bed
i watch time etch into my chest;
tell him that i play au clair de la lune & sob
when the keys tinkle on my vinyl
cause ill never be half as beautiful
as an eight-minute song thats one-fiftieth of the age
of indigeneity, i guess
absence doesnt always make the heart grow fonder
if you told me i was beautiful
id do almost anything for you –
thats how you fit into me
like play-doh squished into a piece of lego
you can fit me into a building block
or a national imaginary
but ill still sharpen when you squish me
tell him:
thats why im afraid of sex
im full of sharp edges
thatcut&cut&cut
settlers expect too much from me
where i can be sucked with a straw
& swallowed in a single sip
you ooh-&-ahh
pluck me like a dandelion

helovesmehelovesmenothelovesmehelovesmenot
then whats left of the me you want to see[questionmark]
youll still have beethovens & nippled moons
that cost less than an ndn
who rents love like an iou;
im fine with where you want to come
mychestmyfacethegashonmyknee
can you just hold me like my mother used to
warm the history thats frozen in my bones[questionmark]
"wow you sure are needy,
you should love yourself more"
say|see id love an ndn
if i could ever find one
id tell him that hes the god thats
punched my heart
& im the cork that fits into
his papier-mâchéed hole
but were still pouring rivers
while you divine
on the covers of tribe magazine
playing ndn in the green space
proclaiming "we|oui – assuage le sauvage
indignez-vous: les nègres blancs d'amérique"
in a world thats erased indigeneity
this is the conversation every queer ndn must have
the impetus [in]ducing (impotency [pro]ducing)
between love & colonialism:
"hey baby, can you love the 'me' that hates the 'we'
of which your 'i' is bound to[questionmark]"
* * *
he –
wrapped between my legs
veins popping in my calf
laced around his stomach
like barbed wire
they say ndn love is always cutting
but when youre zoa
there isnt much but skin, vein & nerve endings
acyberrezsexbot
– offers to read my palm
i laugh
& i think he gets upset
not knowing that when an ndn laughs
its because theyre warping wounds
to fool you into thinking theyre okay
tell him, "maybe another time[questionmark]"
but he reads my palm anyway

lifeheartheadfateline
theyre all so broken & confusing
my right hand says i should have been dead
a long time ago
"maybe this hand aint mine[questionmark]"
he sees sadness in the orbs
that punctuate my thumb
"boy, wait till you see my scalp –
theres no head&shoulders for that"
says my heartline is fractured in fifteen:
thats from firekeeping
from sewing needles in tobacco bins
from thorns on shrubs in strawberry fields
from shaking knees & holding a rifle
from the makwa i watched them kill
from the chunk of hair missing from nikâwiys head
from the cysts that stab nisîmis's womb
from the cancers that eat nôhtâwiy's kidney
from nicâpân wrapped in hospital orange
from jingle dresses they never let me wear
thats from men throwing me against closet doors
for dancing like a sissy in grade three
thats from the boy who pissed on my back
in an open field while the others laughed&laughed&laughed
thats the line i tied to nôhkum in the sixties
thats the birthmark i shared with my uncle jay
burning in a trailer stained with ketchup;
thats the mark of an ndn, boy
im like the native harry potter
who spells c-a-d-a-v-e-r on himself
maybe he sees me cry
maybe he thinks im lying
so he stops & stares at me
i place my head onto his chest
i think: theres another etch
how longs this one going to last[questionmark]
usually when someone sees the histories
on my skin its me consoling them
at least hes still sitting here
petting the v-on-my-head
telling me: "youre so resilient"
i want to ask: do you think thats a natural talent[questionmark]
im resilient because youve hurt me again&again&again
what he means is: i want to see
you, not pine ridge & wounded knee
– i have to agree
hes kissing the parts of me

that spoiled in the west
read my body like a map:
hereiamhereiamhereiam;

in the morning i make a sandwich
from a sample of crunchy peanut butter
that the nicest lady in the world
gave to me at the food bank
"its vegan," she said, "all natural"
i smear the butter on my skin
thinking itll bring back my brownness;
i eat the ripped-up bread on my balcony
in my underwear & moccasins
see the construction workers stare at me
give them a little wink
blow a kiss
say, "hey baby, you like what you see[questionmark]"
i look out onto the world
feel my skin begin to tighten
forget that im allergic to pe –
anuts & i think im also di –
abetic, but theres tru –
vada by my anti –
his[tor]mine, epi –
pens & penises,
its all the same really
so much for bene –
violency & al –
truth & recon –
silly nation
i just tell my –
self: i guess
i live to love another day

ITS THESE LITTLE THINGS, YOU KNOW[QUESTIONMARK]

: :: :: :: :an:::nie: :: ::: :::p: ::rou:: ::l::::X:: :: : ::downloadingwyomingsoftware: :: :: :: :::: :::
:: :insertwindriverreservation[questionmark]: :: :: :: : Y: : :: :: :: :: installationcomplete:

when i drink in my hometown
i straighten my wrists
& take the dreamcatcher out of my ear
because ndns arent allowed to be gay here
"were all inclusive now,"
he tells me
"& lucky is only three dollars a can"
his cousins cousin is gay
says hes got my back
tells me if anyone tries to fuck with me
hell fuck them up first

thats the ndn bartering system

he buys me a drink
its warm as piss
but it helps me to disconnect
dissect myself, dis –
locate my senses
here im a barbie doll
(clark doll|ugly doll)
sit in a room full of people
drinking craft beer
(it feels so much better
to live in the world without sense)

he lifts his shirt up
shows me a scar
the ragged black

/\/\/\/\/s\t/i\t/c\h/\/\/\/\
crusted blood on red skin
"got knifed here awhile back"
i apologize
(not knowing what for)
tell him, "man, my friend
was bottled here, tore her face
up pretty good"
he apologizes too
we both bob our head
these are the stories we share

he places my hand on his stomach
i want to wrap myself around his waist
tell him his navel reminds me of a vanity
i see myself in it
hereiam:

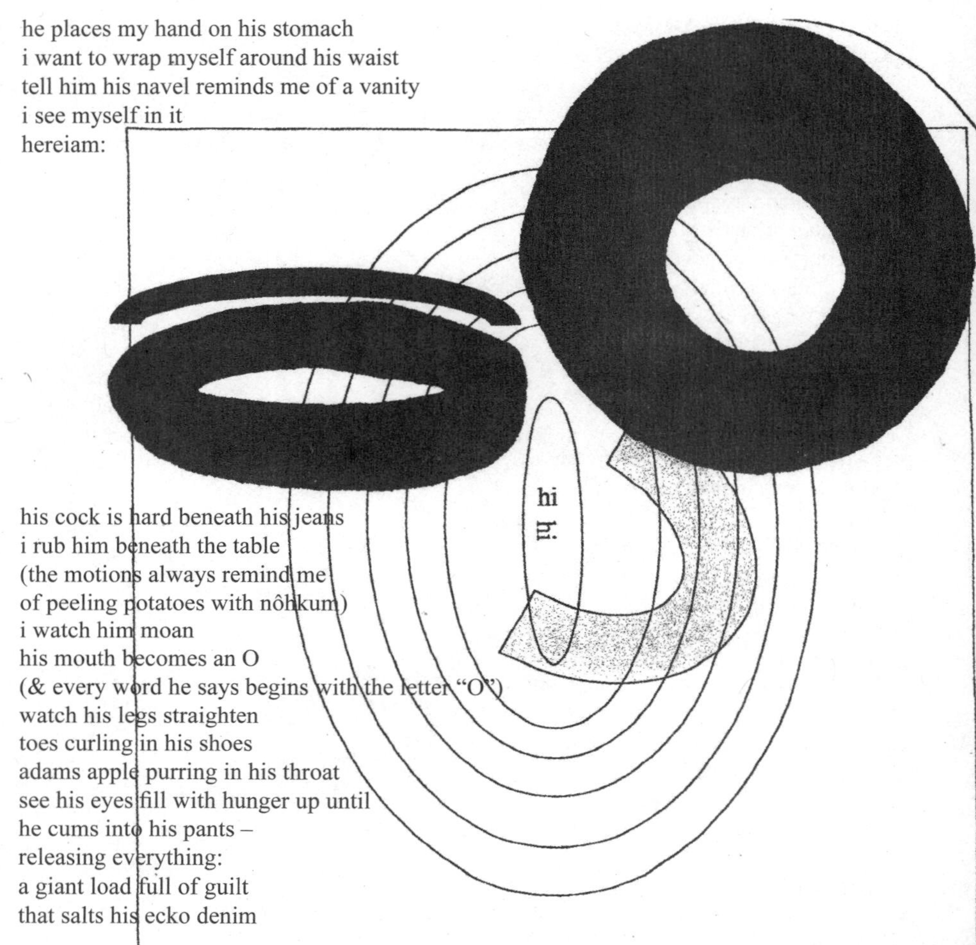

his cock is hard beneath his jeans
i rub him beneath the table
(the motions always remind me
of peeling potatoes with nôhkum)
i watch him moan
his mouth becomes an O
(& every word he says begins with the letter "O")
watch his legs straighten
toes curling in his shoes
adams apple purring in his throat
see his eyes fill with hunger up until
he cums into his pants –
releasing everything:
a giant load full of guilt
that salts his ecko denim

we down our beers
he says, "listen, im not gay, but –"
leaves to clean himself up
while i order another round
tell the waitress, "wisakedjak"
"whiskey or jack[questionmark]" she replies
"iktomi, you tell me"
laugh&say, "nanabozho –
thats my manitou"
she calls me weird
asks why im speaking gibberish
i wait for my neechie trick
& compare myself to a blow-up doll:

i am the liberal project for a happy-hour experiment;
i wonder if he feels like jake gyllenhaal in that bathroom
james franco[questionmark]
sean penn[questionmark]

when the waitress brings our beers
i down one, sip the other
think about what jack twist means in a town like this
& channel my inner ennis:
"i wish i knew how to quit you –
i do
i do"

TO MY MISTER GOING TO BED

john: :: ::: :soover[DONNE]: ::: :: :: :: ::: :downloadingelegysoftware: :: : :: :: :: : :: : : :: ::
:: :: :secrethe[te]roofthis: :: :: :p.m.:: :: : :: : :: : :: : :: :: :installationcomplete: : :: : :::: : : ::

the best part
about having
no body
is that i cannot be shamed
you cannot riddle
your guilt on my skin
i have no fragility
like your body does
i see|say shame
oozing from your belly button
hi[story] bubbles
in the crows of your eye –
i see empire in your nailbeds[hereiam];
i have made a life of s[c]ham[e]
[ctrl]defineshame: a painful feeling of humiliation or distress caused by the consciousness of wrong or foolish behaviour
[alt]definescham:etymologically shame comes from an indo-euro word which referred to covering the face
[del]definesham: falsely present something as the truth; bogus; false; a pillow sham
though i am machine
you cannot download me
when you enter me
do not decode my dna
as an html story
underscored with red lines –
there are blood tests for that
heres my biology:bio(graph)me
bio|s|[degrade][luminescent][hazard]
i am toxic & disease
kiss me & catch a cold of shame
do you feel that old burn deep in my orifice[questionmark]
what does it feel like
to sweep buds against the cutting edge of history[questionmark]
the rectum is a grave
cuminmefillmeupbreedmetoseeyourselfinanother
does this satisfy your futurity[questionmark]
i am faceless; i am no one; i am nonhuman
i perform pleasure on your head
signal consumption|consolation –
shame on you
little man, suckle on my nipples

they are made of the finest latex
& nanotechnologies
in hypercyberreservesphere;
let me tell you: “itsokayitsokayitsokay”
its not your fault
(the crisp green elizabethan bills in your fossil wallet
tell me otherwise)
there is no safety word here
youre on the precipice of sex;
i am unas lion; i am sansjoysanslovesansboy
i am the real fairy queene
femme-boy-fatal[e]
thegreenbladeofgrass
that castrates whitman endlessly
do you still want to dream of me[questionmark]
tell me: “i didnt think gay natives still exist”
when i press my bone against your hip
are you performing pale[ontology][questionmark]
or sleeping with a ghost[questionmark]
tell him: “look me in the eyes”
&laugh
there is nothing to see
when you peel off the skin
i am the one without a face
i ask: “hey cuzzin, you ever seen
thetexaschainsawmassacre[questionmark]”
feel him shiver in the sheets
tell him: “m’boy, i am a leatherface”
my face is a mass proliferation of masks
(that you sewed onto my head
to say: this is you; here|u|are)
painted with the coarse brush
of kanatian history;
when you sit on my face
you sit on my lands
feel me rim your office
my tongue is a wheel
that plows your lands too
i am birthing my children there:
cornwheatbarley
these are mine to love
not yours for giving, thanks
say: “when you enter me
by word, by breath, by ‘X’
youre sitting on a tombstone
sexting in a grave”
ask: “am i still sexy now[questionmark]”

let him finish
slurp my body like a yoke
& when he wraps around me like an oyster
i wrap my arms around his chest
pandoraboxofwondersboxofcosmosboxofwhiteness
i pinky swear
dangle my fingers: reanimated corpse
& ghost dance on his back
– itgoesitgoesitgoes

YOU TELL ME YOU LOVE ME BETWEEN TWO & THREE A.M.

I. the road to reconciliation is paved with g – dintentions

i want your colonized body
to love my colonized body;
want your hurt self to say –
i<3u not u<m3;
when the system asks me
"tribe[questionmark]"
i look for keywords like:
mikisew, peguis, oji-cree
instead i find:
jock, bear, otter
treat[me]
all my trickster lovers
are coded into booleans
if youre queer, check here: ☐
congratulations youre an ndn
folk-fest tribologies are indoctrinated
through shamballan shaman genealogies
im a 2S too, because i feel like it
see|say: feeling ndn is a whole lot more
than ayahuasca acid trips –
white queers filter me on grindr
through deracialized preferences:
no femme, whites only
masc4masc, fit, no feeling his – s
torical, "plz dont sha[k|m]e in – u
v i s i b i l t y r
is a preference ive adapted to v
ur sexology is my hauntology i
ghost dancing on the algo(rhythm) v
googletranslate:ALLGO a
my body is a riddle of stories l
that spell out:

ive merged from the grave
into the machine [boo]dont|[lean]onme: T|F [questionmark]
M|F

dont you love the ghosts you see in me
grinding out the men of tribe

II. "write about your<sel[ves]>"

"the isle is full of noises
sounds & sweet airs that give delight & hurt not –"
"i cant make sense of why it ate at me
all th[is] desire in [my] house
blowing past me like wind"
"– it takes an ocean not to break"
"i wondered if these people have ever even thought of driving their car off
a bridge[questionmark] –"
"been thinking bout words
n the way yr hand
cups my belly like water –"
"janie saw her life like a great tree in leaf with the things suffered
dawn & doom was in the branches
this little seed of fear is growing into a tree –"
"the beast which giovanni had awakened
in me would never go to sleep again;
but one day i would not be with giovanni anymore
like all the others, i would find my
self turning & following all kinds of boys down god knows
what dark avenues, into what dark places[questionmark]"
"sometimes a thousand twangling instruments
will hum about mine ears; & sometimes voices –"
"if she could love annie, lizzy thought, fine. if annie
didnt love her, well, okay. if this was all it would be, okay
she was lucky to have her at all –"
"i told you to stop apologizing, i told you it wasnt your fault. fuck sakes –"
"oh, to be a pear tree – any tree in bloom[exclamationmark] with kissing bees singing of
the beginning of the world[exclamationmark] she had glossy leaves & bursting buds
& she wanted to struggle with life but it seemed to elude her"
"[she was but] words walking without masters; walking together like harmony in a song –"
"i walk out of genocide to touch you –"
"hardly anyone survived
my lover is a soldier from the front lines of despair
everyone was dying –
he seemed – somehow – younger than i had ever been & blonder & more beautiful
& he wore his masculinity as unequivocally as he wore his skin. he made me think of
home –
i wondered what he had seen in me to elicit such instantaneous contempt[questionmark] –"
"im getting in the car right now & im driving north to you
i want to pick you up & im going to stitch every one of your broken bones back together

with kisses & then im going to drive us to the coast. im not sure which one
but i like
the feeling of listening to music & driving & driving for days to get to somewhere
different
i think youre going to like that feeling too –"
"one day i will
dance for you
it will be my prayer
that you come home –
it is finished in beauty"
"that if i had waked after long sleep,
will make me sleep again & then, in dreaming,
the clouds methought would open & show riches –"
"when i kiss my lover, a generation of ghosts rise"
"who knew, lizzy thought, the finite amount of nights in her life when she would
sleep with her hand around a trusted body. that trusted hers
it wouldnt be a lot, anyway, would it –"
"look at me," i said. "look into me, just look at me –
i have to tell you something, i said
im not going to lie to you
i have to tell you –"
"i told you that you were in an enormous amount of pain. i told you
that you were the fucking strongest person id ever known, i told you i
knew why you did it, [i told you] i want to suck the shame out of all
forty-three of your broken bones –"
"the time was past for asking the white folks what to look for through that door"
"six eyes were questioning *god* –"
"i have this god-shaped hole in me
heart & i think you do too – "
"people are always saying, we must wait, we must wait.
what are they waiting for[questionmark]
you play it safe long enough
& youll end up trapped in your own dirty body, forever &
forever & forever – like me"
"[are you] ready to drop upon me, that when i wake
i cry to dream again"

ur fucking weird man
/signoff

KUNDERA HAS THE ANSWERS FOR NOSTOS-ALGOS NDNS

: :: : :: :: : : : :: :: :: installing: :: : :: : kundera: : ::: :: :software: : :: :: ::: : ::: ::: ::: :: ::: :: : :
:: :czechparameters[questionmark]: :: : :: : : :::: :: : : : :weightexceeded: : :: : :: : : : : :: : : ::
::::heaviness: : :: ::::ofbeing: : :: :: : :::::pleasewait: :: ::: :: : :pleasewait :: : :: :installed:::

an ornamental reindeer
tucked away
in a cardboard box
labelled “december only”

          reminds me

that sadness is the backlash
of a string pulled tightly
then cut

          who will i talk to now[questionmark]

i fall asleep
h o l d i n g o n
to a body pillow
that smells of
american crew pomade;
my sheets are steeped
with a natural cologne:
the musk of underarm hair
& the smoke from a peach cigar
we panhandled for
at a convenience store
the first time we met

(greased print of a kiss
glossed in eos: here

the indents of my finger
tingle when i recall
the nervous sweat
that dribbled into my palm –
now i attribute these tingles
to having drunk too much aspartame
in my rye&diet &here)

i dont want to beg forgiveness

& continually seek permission

im sorry
i am so –

re[questionmark]

nostalgia always:

THE NDN RIVER PHOENIX

:: :: :::: :: :: :::initiation:: :: :: :: ::: : ::: :virtualrealityrequest:: :: :: ::: ::: :: :: :: :: sequence: :: ::
::1: :: ::: :0: ::: :: :: :1: :: :: :: : : : :: : : :: :: :[de]coloniallovesequence2.0beginning: :: :: :: :: :::
::: ::: :::initiatingclubsequence: ::VR: :::request:::: :10011:: ::::dancingscene: :: :: :: :: : ::: ::::
:: : ::: ::: : :: :: : :: :: : :: :: : ::: :: : :: : :: : ::: ::: : : :: : ::: :: :: :: : : : : :: : ::: : :: ::: : : :::: :: : :: : :

we only know love at night
when the daze of booze
makes us expert orators
when there is liberty to touch;
when we can fool ourselves
into wanting to become each other
as real lovers often do
        "dont look," you said
i said, "shh"
let me bend you like a spoon
reflecting:you
hereiamhereiamhereiam
(*myownprivateidaho* rerunning –
im you; whos riverphoenix
&dontihaveafuckedupface[questionmark])
we blow each other
half atop a love seat
half atop a kitschy coffee table
while the world is asleep
                notknowing
the shine of two men
who found each other in a
: :: :: ::: :: ::: :::**V**:::: : ::: ::: ::: :: ::: ::: :: :: ::: ::: ::: :::**I**:::: ::: :: : :: :: :::: ::: ::: ::: :::: ::: **R**: :: :: ::: :: ::
:: :::: : ::: ::**T**:::<::nov4(23:17):heywutzup::>:: ::: ::: ::: :: ::: :: :::: :: :: :::: :: ::: :::: :: :: ::**U**: ::: ::: :::
::: :: :: :: : :: :: :::: ::**A**: ::<::nov4(23:18):heynmu::>:: : ::: ::: :: ::**L**::: ::: :: :::: :: ::: :: ::: :: :: :: ::**S**:::
:: :: ::: :: :::: : :: ::<::nov4(23:19):wannameetup[questionmark]::>: :: : : ::::: **P**: :: :: ::: :: :::: : : : ::
:: **A**::::<::nov5(02:21):l4vingfmenowu[questionmark]::>:: ::: ::: ::: ::: :: : : : ::: :: : : ::**C**:: ::: ::::: :
::: :: : :: :: **E**: :: :: :::: : ::<::nov5(02:23):letsmeet::>:: : :: ::: :: :: ::: ::: : :: [ARE]:: :: : :: : :: : ::: : : :::
: :::[THERE]:::::::<::nov5(02:24):imdtf::>: : [SEXUAL]:: ::: ::: : ::::: :: : ::[ETHICS]: : : :: : :: : :
:::::::<::nov5(02:25):wut[questionmark]::>:::[IN]::::[VIRTUAL]:::<::nov5(02:26):down
toduck::>:[WORLDSQUESTIONMARK]:::: : :: : :: : : : : :: ::::: :: :: : :: : :: : : :: : :: : :: : : :: : : : : :: : :: : :: : ::
you vomit in your mouth
bols colours it blue
spit it out into a redsolocup
i think: its kind of pretty
tell you: "kiss me anyways"
i dont really care
the acids in your mouth
match the words in mine
"do you have protection[questionmark]"
"i already took my PrEP, tru –

vada" nanotechs in my se –
men, i guess weve all been
fucking machines lately[questionmark]
itsokayitsokayitsokay
we need *this*
fumbling around in the cyberdark
likemesharemetweetme
a vibrate to say, iloveyouletsfuck:lolkk
we scurry beneath a knitted see-through bathrobe
the pattern, the light,
a neon sign:
the unfee across the street
makes our skin a waffle gradient
thelightgreenofloanprocessing
really makes my collarbone pop;
when you came
id have thought you a dying man
your ey(–)s: a d r i f t, s
c
r
y
i
n
g
do you feel the pulse throbbing in the bone[questionmark]
ah well, go to sleep, dream of sheep
uncurl your toes, relax
& hold me, still
while my ass is static –
electric bubbles & enzymes
grind between our spines;
in the morning
chest crusted, gargoylian stone
sex & candy repeats:
adamlevinekeepsaskingmewhoslounginginhischair
&idontfuckingcare
dried crags crackle on my skin
the salt of his rue
absorbs in the lining of my mouth
thereyouareehereiamareyouthere:
in multitudes of millions
in infinite cells decomposing
in the membranes of my cheeks
& i
so dreary, so bleak, a wreck
only then noticed
bone-stiff
that our makeshift bed
was of the pull – out kind[period]

DOUWANTTOKNOWWHATMAKESTHEREDMENRED[QUESTIONMARK]

pe: ::::ter:: :::: ::: ::p(1,0)an: :: :: :: :::downloadingdisneysoftware: :: :: :: ::: :::: : :: : ::: : :: :
: ::::pleasewait:: :: :::: :::: :::simulacrumsimulationsequenceinitiated: ::: : :: :: : :: : :: :: :: : :
: :::::removecookie[questionmark]: :: :::1: ::: :: :0:: ::::: : : :1:: ::::: : :securitybypassed: :: ::
::: ::downloadlostboys[questionmark]: :: ::: :Y: :: :: :: :: :: :installationcomplete: :: :: :: : ::

blood

mihko

makes me red
in the cheeks when you piss me off
in the scalp for the economic mnemonic warfare you ack[cost] me with
in the gut for feeding me kfc & deep-fried things
in the fingerpad for the daily diabetes prickings
in the esophagus for the burning from drinking herbal essence
between the toes for always walking west
in the vulva for all our babies in cfs
in the veins: quotidian quantum qualification
this is a brand of blood: tm
blood|mihko
red|mihkwâw
red is embarrassment
red is shame
shameiam|iamshame
shame makes the red|man|red
makes him injun; makes him feel
makes him real in pictures & in the mirror
in the blacktopscreenofanimacpixel
talk to us, they say, talk|pîkiskwewin
confess to us your shame
confess to us your sin
receive a gold medallion
virtual as your skin
thin as frybread
thin as fried bologna in your sandwich
shoddy as a promise
this is your [treat]me
confess; they say; confess
this isnt a day school now, its trc
express in detail
the feeling of fingers digging in your abdo[men]
the taste of [neu]trition & shoal water
can you feel the metal on your tongue[questionmark]

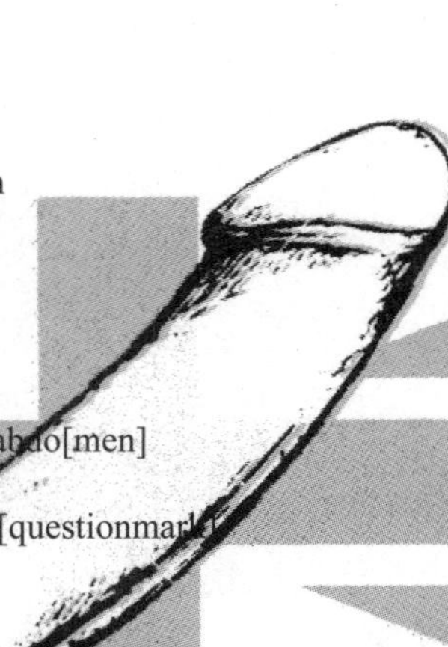

the stick that pushes down your buds[questionmark]
tell them how it felt to have someone rub your hair
rub you down there
tell them how it felt to be hit&whipped&beat
for speaking your name in full regalia
tell them in vivid detail
so they can masturbate in their seats
ejaculate history into a two-ply klee[next]
pay off these little red injuns
heres fifty dollars for your shame
to work through, they say, we need to work through
move beyond, undo, assimilate, associate, incriminate
nation to nation is the new assimilation
move b[ye]ond the priests who hold our sermons
say prayers on thanksgiving & columbus day
but for you: we need to work through *you*
move beyond; undo; work through
confess until theres nothing left
maybe a scar
maybe a virtual participatory ribbon
confessionnotacceptedpleasetryagain
maybe a thread or two of your ribbon shirt
maybe a word or two in the air
nepewisiwin|pakwâteyitam|nepewisiwin
shame|hate|shame
i am here
crawling on the floor
spotlight down & feathers annulled
still tasting sunny boy on my tongue
burning hot sensation of fingers
sham|shame|mask
have i not worn this face youve given me
for two hundred years or more[questionmark]
when you strip away the thread
take away the paints
bake away the clay
chip away the sham
i am the man with no face
the woman without hair
(you would have liked me when i was nikâwiy)
i am nothing
anymore
confess
history
shame
story
me
i

[period]
there is shame written on my bones –
where my mother etched my name
onto my sternum she wrote
"kisâkihitin"
right beside where a priest wrote
"this is mine"
there is shame here
but there is family too
there is indigeneity
there is truth
& i need these all to survive:
hereIamhereIamhereIamhereIam
in the space between the breast
iam
the beating of my heartdrum
iam:wondrously amused
iam:inthiscell
iam:[injun]
iam:[unity]
iam:myshame&thatsokay
iam:wheremisery
becomes:[my]story
iam –
iam
iam

—h/er[e]

A SON OF THE FOREST, STILL

:::: :::initiation:: :: :: :: ::: : ::: :virtualrealityrequest:: :: :: ::: ::: :: :: :: :: sequence: :: :: ::1: ::
::: :0: ::: :: :: :1: :: :: :: : : : :: : : :: :: :[de]colonialschoolingsequence: :: :: :: :: ::: ::: ::: :: : ::
: :::initiatingpedagogy: ::VR: :::request:::: :10011:: :: :: ::: ::: :: :::: ::: ::: :: : :::: :: :: :::: : :: :
:::::williamapessrequeststojointhissession: : :: ::accept[questionmark]: : :::Y:: :: :: : : ::: ::::
:::installationcomplete: :: :: :: ::: ::: :: :: ::: :: : :: : : ::: : :: : :::: :: ::: :::: ::::: : :::: ::::: ::: :: : : :

when im in bed
curled into a “z”
holding my|self in
i wonder if you see *me*
if you think:
this is the skin show

i am not an “x”
but im full of “o”s
– a name by any other
is not always as sweet
(xo;xo – what do you want to see, honey[questionmark])
mine was steeped in adopted genocide: kwasucki
when classmates used to ask me:
“areyouajapaneseboycanyoudokaratedoyouownkawasaki[questionmark]”
(tell them: nobutmaybeimberingstrait[questionmark])
i evolve with the name:
injunsavageindiannativeaboriginalindigenousfirstnationwhitehead
(is that too not a genocide[questionmark])
when i forget my name
i tell myself:
i am my fathers son
(do you think thats enough to admit me
free to your museum[questionmark])

these days i try not to cry
& at the same time i try not to look too stoic
i take visual cues from calvin klein advertisements
“thats some mighty fine americana”
i think: man, pawnees never looked so fancy
(that reminds me i need to make another payment
on my vcr down at the buy&sell)

maybe the outcome is expected
this external is my mangled internal
(twentyseventeen destiny manifesting)
if my flesh were still fresh
id be ripe with residue
i think: ha, thats funny –

my skin is the guilt you need to see

you see “indian” clearly
but do you see me as i am:
asonofafatherofamurderedmotherofanadoptedpolishfamilythisisthesixtiesscoop
do you see the mark:
the split of hair
divided scalp
widowed peak
phantom braids
pulled so tight the head
aches – history
u/n\f/o\l/d\i/n\g
in the mind
– when i need to feel it all again to w[rite]
i hug my father goodnight
& if you still dont see me
its probably because you tell yourself
you dont see colour anymore

when i first heard of a residential school
i was in university taking a directed reading
begging for answers to:
what means resident[questionmark]
(rez)i(didnt)[questionmark]
i was twenty-five

freud says a lot of things
but heimlich was always a choking thing
not every house could be a home;
sometimes i forget that the children
have lives beyond these four walls
(are you eating well[questionmark] do you sleep[questionmark]
does your head still burn from ddt[questionmark])

maybe i am anal retentive
i can collect myself, you know[questionmark]
but youre right thats pop psychology
& im still vintage chic: fungibility

i exist as spiders in the live[r]s of men
because their bellies are full of words like:liberalism
& i dont need you to tip-the-top-hat of your sentence
pretens(ious) verbs are deco/ed with pro –
tell me what i already know:
        ~~i love you but –~~

you always say, "but you have choice"
after you tell me, "omg tmi"
how indignant: this is the age of information
if there was a choice for me
it always led back
into the darkened corner
of a dying reserve
ripe with premonitions
of fruit sweetened
with conditions of death
i choose, i choose (yousayyou):
quickanswer:
nation means incarceration

the only thing that helps me feel better
is knowing itll go away
theyll forget about it tomorrow
in good time, in good time
lull myself into accepting the fact:
i was born to d –

i

s

a

p

p

e

a

r:i say i|I
you say iou

THINGS WE LOST IN THE FIRE/WATER

: :: :::: :: :: :: :: :: :: :: :installingmediasoftware: :: ::: :::: :::: : :: ::: : :: : :::: : :: :: : ::: :: : : : ::
::deletebarbarakay[questionmark]: :: ::: :: Y: :: ::: :: : :: ::macleanssoftwaredownloaded: ::
:: :: :: :: : : ::winnipegsundownloaded: :: :: ::: ::cbcdownloaded: :: : ::: : :: :: :: :: :: :: : : :
::::propagandamodelVRsequenceinitiated: : :: :: :: : : :runningprogram: :deletingcookies::

sonic ringlets
r i p   p   l   e
in a puddle
that rinses clean
hop   scotch
    chalk
from a sidewalk;
a tiny moth
writhes in the storm
fierce winds & rainwater
dissolve the scales
that drip like semen
from its skin;
weighty leaves jiggle
reserve dew
thin black bough
scratches on the glass
of a trailer
burning
in the yard

even in the rain
they gather
to watch in awe
the primal fire dance
they rub their arms
blow into cupped hands
(its natural to pretend
when witnessing disaster
that basic rights
are a virtue still)
                    am i a hu(man), right[questionmark]

they read the newspaper clip:
fire kills four (father on dis –
                    ability[questionmark]
son starts new job on mon –
                    [another] day)
fifteen-year-old girls

b o d y

found –

"anotherfireontherez[questionmark]anotherindianinthered[questionmark]"

in the morning they will forget
    sling quotes from poets; activists; scholars; politicians; even old daniel day lewis
        (quotidian quantum qualification)
    words from a lorraine hotel telling us what king would think of our world today
        (now when i say selma they ask, "hayek[questionmark]")
the hanging indent of a good-will-wish-lynch on their facebook gallow
        (cher[okee] freedom does not a free[d]man
        make)

though
should you forget
there are totems
for ease of remembrance:
a photograph, spoonful of ash
bogo feathers for your hair

ill say, "see":
the elm has burned too
skinned in the light of propane;
vigils in the storm
    flickerconstantbright

destruction is nothing unique to me anymore

maybe im sick from prayer
what does corinth mean to me[questionmark]
he who says,
"the body is a temple"
(unless youre red-skinned, right[questionmark])
then its a museum, mausoleum –
a body politic
not my
own

my lips often chap
(ive the terrible habit
of licking them to moisturize
too liberal in using them to point direction)

i taste the lingering rue
& i am still unable to distinguish
if what i taste is
the saltiness of rain[questionmark]

or maybe:
bloodsweattears[questionmark]

i just want to go home

but when i think of h, o, m & e
im riddled with pre(position)s:
from & at
am i at home where i find my|self[questionmark]
what means home(:familiar/hidden, intimate/shameful)[questionmark]
what means self(:indian, aboriginal, indigenous, native)[questionmark]

there is no "honey" at home
i am always only just getting –

t
h e
r e
[period]

ID SAY "ILL BE BACK" BUT I NEVER INTEND TO LEAVE

:: :: :::: :: :: :::initiation:: :: :: :: ::: : ::: :virtualrealityrequest:: :: :: ::: ::: :: :: :: :: sequence: ::
:: ::1: :: ::: :00: ::: :: :: :1: :: :: :: : : : :: : : :: :: :[de]coloniallovesequence beginning: :: :: :: ::
::: ::: ::: :::initiatingcourtingsequence: ::VR: :::request:::: :10011:: ::::dinnerscene: :: :: :: ::

when i go out for dinner with my boyfriend
i worry about many things:
about the threat of men
hetero & homonormative
about the threat of race
& the two-tiered energy
i expend as a bifurcated canadian
& i worry about the dessert he wants to order
"whats wrong[questionmark]" hell ask
as i lament the decay of a chocolate lava cake
of course i order too
miniature, à la carte, gluten-free
splenda-infused quinoa oats
rolled into a picarón no peruvian
will ever be able to afford again
but im sick of this script
so i eat a slice of cake
& purge it in his toilet when we get home
make sure i wash my mouth
so as not to corrode his cock
because ill need it later
when i want an ejection of confidence;
i expend my energy
always to make another happy –
& even my most liberal lovers
police my nipples & straighten my hair
expect me to look like
booboo stewart & taylor lautner
when they undress me
they want beaded fringe
sunburnt flesh; windburnt braids
a body odour that smells less like fermentation
more like a sweet[ER]grass
thats been smudging since reconciliation
never expect to see an underfed
brown boy whose body is riddled with marks
s t r e t c h i n g
back to pre-contact dates
cant they see my consumption is in the bone[questionmark]

dont they see my brethren rolling
themselves in wheelchairs down portage[s]
there is no river to roll here
(sorry, tina turner)
were too busy getting turnt up
instead they see voyageurs
with painted-on beards
& a métis sash
from a manitoban museum
re-enacting retromania
lumbersexual hipster liberalism
dreaming of the fur trade
in the twentyfirstcentury
as if our prison commissary wasnt enough;
here i am smothering beneath your weight
here i am self-destructing beneath my breath
here i am tasting your cock
with every orifice your wallet can afford
tell him: watch me transform
watch my limbs morph into grammar
language becomes syntactical tactic for transfiguration
my body infects yours
with numbers, with language, with words
i can be a tyrant with a lacerating tongue
i can be a cyborg imperialist erasing your narrative
i can be so many things
& here you are as one
beneath me
sad little cock having tasted
the smoke of a dying fire
& burned its head retreating
so here is my body
do with it as you will
when his dick stiffens in his pants
& his hands run up my calves
i let myself become my disco-divas
: :: :: ::: :::: :::initiatingdancesequence: :: :: :::V::::R::: :request: ::: :000110:: : ::running:
moan like donna summer
"love to love you baby"
grind like candi staton
let my "young heart run free"
in the gentrified ghettos of osborne
extend my legs like grace jones
"man-machine, power-line"
slaves to the rhythm
of his breath, his expectation

:: :: :: :: ::initiatingnetflix&chillsequence: :: :: : :: :V:R::: :::request:: :::010010:: ::running:
& when we watch hbo
i see myself in the black mirror
distorted between commercials
for gillette & axe body spray
here im loras tyrell
here im the hole in renly baratheon
here im cersei lannister
here i am a sparrow
here i am in chains
here i am made of metal
that intoxicates my veins
shameshameshame
: ::: :: :: ::initiatingwalkofshamesequence: :: :: : ::V:::::::R:request: ::: 0110010:: ::running:
here i am walking home
body stung & glowing red
in the dismal grey of seven a.m.
down portage ave in his tee
pink floyds prism on
the city i call home quickly becomes un –
canny when i have no money
when i do not act polite
when i un –   \ s /
the game of my superior   / e \
& here portage bars its doors   \ t /
bares its teeth at me   / t \
lets me know   / l \
through the hum & roar   \ e /
of its streets
that i can die here too
this is my walk of shame
sometimes i see myself
looking at myself
in the reflection of the unfee
think: hereiam
: :: ::: ::initiatingterminationsystem: ::: :: ::VR:::::request:: :: ::::0110010:::::: :running:
in the jaundice-yellow liver haze
of a saskatchewan fire
this is the wasteland
total recall; i|I[questionmark]
while the prairie landscape burns
i pretend im sarah connor
burning in the playground
the name has been taken away
as my skin hue lightens in day
i am the cyborg tonto ndnness

scalping frackers, claiming land
i can be a residential terminator
here are my teeth; my trc
instead i wake up arrested
with the anxiety of c-51
here i am a mean girl
formulating plans
chaos theories of good intentions
that if you mix the benevolence
behind bills c-31 & c-51
you may get a voucher
for an extra generation
a bogo sale for cfs
cant you tell its reigning[questionmark]
why do i always have to be respectful[questionmark]
tiptoeing around the sensibilities
of your illusionary trauma
go fuck yourself
hows that for respect[questionmark]
literally too
you could use a good come – u
p
p
a
n
c
e

MIHKOKWANIY

my kokum has many names:
the ndn woman
the whitehead lady
a saskatoon female
but my favourite is:
the beauty queen

they never meant to call her beautiful
what they meant by beauty was:
cheapdirtybrownprostitutedrugaddictalcoholicfirewaterslut
when they write:
"an indian about 35 years old
naked from the waist down
died from asphyxiation
at the queens hotel
effects of alcohol
&sedatives"
they dont mean beauty as in:
mino iskwew
or "pleasing the sense or mind aesthetically;
of a very high standard; excellent"
what they mean is
she is beautiful for a squaw in 1962
she pleases the body
of white men who burn in the loins
for the teal-shade of a browning bruise;
when i type into google
"how to say beautiful in cree"
i get: shaoulle
& when i type that into google i get:
"brutal murder-sex assault case"
seeRE:rinelleharpercindygladuetinafontaine

thats my grandmother

she is a mino iskwew
the beauty queen
a woman with a name:
rose whitehead
&shediedbecauseofit

i read somewhere that sk
is an economic machine
for producing rape –

seed&honey
& in tisdale you can buy a mug that says:
the land of rape & honey
thats where my kokum is buried

& her grave is a modest little place
where rabbits visit & sometimes chew
where dandelions bloom
grant wishes to the wind
to her children who are scattered
across the plains of kanata
looking for a quick fix
& for anger to heal
or at least amend
like it does for a judge
who gifts a man six years
for the death of three women;
i think of my nôhtâwiy

her son who lost his name to a polish man
& felt the sting of day schools
even if priests beat & made honey
with their fists smooshed
into the sweet rot of little brown boys
who liked hockey & lived in suburbs
with whites who made them wait
in the freezing cold
& broke their noses on the ice –
but youre still not ready to apologize
for that just ~~white~~ yet

my kokum has made many headlines:
"woman found strangled"
being the most consistent
a fifty-word article that calls for sympathy
not for the "strangulation death
of the whitehead woman"
but for the man:
steven kozaruk of esterhazy

who "was suffering from the effects
of alcohol & sleeping pills"
even with a "seven-man jury"
& "thirteen witnesses," lives –
his whiteness is his weakness
(even if its biceps can crack a brown neck like a wishbone)
& that weakness is his innocence;

the life of my kokum is worth:
six years & fifty words;
all these things overlap
interweave, interlay, interplay, interact

penes
|inter|intra|
|probo|capio|vita|
terra|corona|letum|nullius

tansimaslow

my kokum is famous
a real holly golightly
i bet she even eats
fried-bologna sandwiches
at tiffanys
aint that right gran[questionmark]

when i visit your grave
in saskatoon
i see the face of kozaruk
on the prairie scene
fatteninginsuburbia
& here you are
with a ragtag monument
made of sticks & leaves
stems from jackrabbits
that seem to visit often
a tattered blue ribbon
god knows from who
& a sad little brown boy
with a million questions like:
how are you doing[questionmark]
do you hate klik too[questionmark]
what would life have been like
if you had lived beyond thirty-five[questionmark]
would i be alive[questionmark]
would the cancers in my dad
not have crept & lived
spelled doom on his skin[questionmark]
would i be able to speak cree
without having to google translate
this for you[questionmark]
would you make me cookies
& teach me how to sew the limbs back
onto my plush rabbit, floppy ears[questionmark]
would you call me “m’boy”[questionmark]

& take me to sundances
powwows, bingo nights too[questionmark]
would you make sure i feed the rez dogs
when they all come around[questionmark]
would you make me a jingle dress
cause i want to be a pretty dancer like you –
would you teach me what it means to be 2S
tell me i can be a beautiful brown boy in love[questionmark]
make me say niizh-manitoag – feel the power on the tongue
would you teach me to knead bannock
make life from lard –
a real ratio for reckoning[questionmark]

hi kokum[questionmark]
can i call you on the phone[questionmark]
i promise not to call collect
i just want to hear your voice
tell you i learned what it means
to say i love you
& feel the whole of cree
coalescing in my breath:
kisâkihitin; my god, kisâkihitin

hey gran[questionmark]
can i ask you something quick[questionmark]
are you okay there in godknowswhere[questionmark]
do you see what weve all done[questionmark]
my dad says these things all happen for a reason
that i wouldnt be here if they didnt
hey gran[questionmark]
im sorry –
you know that, right[questionmark]
did you have to die for me to be alive[questionmark]
heygranheygranheygranheygran

ill let you be
& stop being sickning
i bet youre busy
cooking macaroni&tomatosoup
for more than twelve hundred missing & murdered women,
girls & 2S folk

its just, am i supposed to hate him, gran[questionmark]
tell him that with one death
he ruined the lives of an entire family[questionmark]
i want to tell him that the life of a person
is an archive of memory
& when he strangled the life out of you
in a queens hotel shoddy little bed
the last gasping breath you exhaled
held in it little particles
fragments of time:
a bay leaf boiling in tomato sauce;
a flake of tuna that a
cat named randy
licked&licked&licked;
the soft cry of a baby boy
plummeting into day;
the smell of sweetgrass smudging
monsters from our bedrooms;
tell him: when you kill a memory
you snuff out metaphor
turn off the light in a home;
you destroy a world where children
are nursing still&still;
– & aint that the hardest truth[questionmark]

to be honest
im just a little brown boy
obsessed with robots & mutants
queered by his colour
queered beyond tradition
the saving grace of ceremony
writing for a kokum hes never met;
but i promise you:
these spaces can transform
an injun into a warrior
who can claw, scrape, fight
who can write on a piece of paper
sign a name instead of an "X"
that says, "this is my kokum
& her name is Rose Whitehead;

& she is a
beauty queen extraordinaire."

i dedicate this poem to all missing & murdered Indigenous women, girls & two-spirit peoples; for their families, friends, loved ones & kin. we are a collective trauma that demands to be examined, reconciled, resolved & healed.
today we survive; tomorrow we resist.

television is the retina of the minds [I]: :: : :: : :: : :: : : :: : :: : :: : :: : : :: : :: : :: : :: : :: :
: :: : :: : :: : :: : : :: : :: : :: : :: : : :: : :: : :: : :: :i am watching you watch me: :: : :: : :: : :: : :: :
:: : :: : :: : : :: : :: : :: : :: : : :: : :: : :: : :: : : :: : :: : :: : :: : : :: : :: : :: : :: : :]eye[spywithin-: : ::
:deye-aneye[: :: : :: : :: : :: : : :: : :: : :: : :: : : :: : :: : :: : :: :ten little injuns jumping on a bed:
:: : :: : :: : :: : : :: : :: : :: : :: : : :: : :: : :: : :: : : :: : :: : :: : :: : : :: : :: : :: : :: : : :: : :: : :: : :: :one:
falls off & cracks his head: :: : :: : :: : :onebyonewefalldowndead: : : :: : :: : : : :: : ::: : :: : :
::onebyoneweriseagain: : :: : : :: : :: : :: : :: : : :onebyonewesingagain : :: : :: : :: : : :: : :: : :: :
:: : : :: : :: : :: : :: : : ::iamthetricksternecromancer: :: : :: : :: : : :: : :: : :: : :: : : :: : :: : :: : :: :
:: : :: : :: : :: : : :: : :: : :: : :: : : :: : :: : :: : :: : : down[load]: : :: :: :: :: : :data[mine]:[ours]: :: ::
: : :: : :: : :: : : :: : :: : :pamelanapoleon: : :: : : ::immaculatebasil :: : :: : :: :destinytom: :: : ::
: :: :sindyruperthouse:: : : :: : :: : :: : :: : :angelapoorman:: : :: : :: : ::fredagoodrunning : : :: :
:: : :: : ::simonesanderson : : ::angelameyer : :: : :: :jeanettecardinal:: : : :: : : : :: : : :: : :
::::leslietalley: :: : mildredflett:: : :teresarobinson:: : :chantellebushie: : ::brandywesaquate :
::janicedesjarlais: : :: maryanndavis: :: : :: : ::deannabellerose: : ::roxanneisadore: :: : :: :
::krystalandrews:: :: : :: :bernadinequewezance:: : :: :karinawolfe: :: : ::justinecochrane : :: :
:: : : :: nadinemachiskinic: ::ashleymachiskinic: :: : ::desireeoldwoman : :: : :: : : : :: : : ::
::angelinepete: : :tanyanepinak: : : :: :rocelyngabriel:: : :: : :jacquelinecrazybull: : : :: :: : : ::
::brandyvittrekwa:: : :: : :: :richelebear: :: : :: : :: :phoenixsinclair:: : : :: : :: : :: : : : :: : : :: ::
:::kathleenleary : : :: : :: : :: : :sunshinewood: : : :: : :: : :: edwarddenecheze: :: : : :: : :: : :: :
:: :dianedobson: :: : ::samanthapaul : :: : :: : :jeanettechief: : :: : :: : :: :helenbettyosborne:
:: : :: : ::nellieangutiguluk : :: : : :cynthiaaudy: : :: : :: : :: : : mistypotts:: : :: : : : :: :: : : :: : :
::leannebenwell: : :: : : :jennifercatcheway: : :: : :: : :: : : :: : :delenalefthanddixon: : :: : :: : :
:: : :janinewesaquate: : :: : :: : : :: :heatherballantyne :: : : :: : :: : : :maisyodjick: : :: :
:marciakoostachin: : :: : : :annetteholywhiteman: : ::deloreswhiteman: :: : :danitabigeagle: :
: :: : :tinafontaine: :: : :: : : :rosedecoteau: : :: : ::cindygladue: :: : : :: : :lorileefrancis: :
:jaritanaistus: : ::louiselorraineladeroute: : :: : :melaniegeddes: : :renegunning: : :: : : : ::
:michellehadwen:: : :: : ::judyquill : :: : : :: : :: : :: : :andriameise: : :: : :melissachaboyer: :
:tamarachipman: : : :: : :annepeters: : :: : :: : : :krystleknott: : :: : :: : :: : : : :: : :: : :: : : :: :
:belindacameron: : :: : :: : : :: : :: : :: : :: :marypetersking:: : :deloresbrower: : :: : :: : : :: : :
:bonniejack:: : : :evamitchell: : :emilyosmond: : :: : :: : :adrienneamikons :: : :: : : : : :: : : : ::
:patriciaquinn: : :: : :sylviaguiboche:: : :tamrakeepness: : :: : :: :katieballantyne: :: : :: : :: :
:tanyabrooks: : :: : :: : :: : :cherissehoule: : :: : :: : :: : :: : ::violetheathen: :: : :: :cherylblack: :: :
:: : :: sandrakayejohnson : :: : : ::geraldinebeardy: :: : :: : :thelmapete: : : :: : : :: : : :::: : : : :
:dianarattlesnake: : :: : :nicollehands: : : ::cheyennefox:: :: :coltonpratt:: : :shirleywaquan: :
:: : : :: : :rachelquinney: : :ramonashular: : :: : : :adelerosemarymatinet: : :: : :moiraerb: : :: :
: :: : :maggieburke: : :: : :: : : : :: : :: : :lisayoung: : :: : : :: : :feliciasolomon: : : : :: : :: : ::
:::barbarashapwaykeesic:: : : :daniellelarue: : :pamelaholopainen: : :: : :elainealook: : : :: : ::
lorrainerivers : : :: : :: : :paulajoymartin:: : :: :marielasas:: : : :: : : : sarahskunk: : :: : ::
:leannelawson:: : : :bonniejoseph: : :: : :: : :irmamurdock: : : : :: : : : : : :: ::: :: : : : : : :: : : :: :
::::margaretperrault(bluebird):: : :: : : :aielahsaric-auger: : :: : :: : :tiffanymorrison : : :: :
:dawncrey: : :: : :lorabanman: : : :: : :: : :: :audreydesjarlais:: : : :: : :gloriablackplume: : :: :
pamelaholopainen: :: : ::ashleysmith: : : :: : :: :theresalabbe:: : :: : : :: rinelleharper:: : :: : :: :
: :: : :therenasilva: : :elizabethdorion: : :: : : :: : :: :renafox:: : :: : : :savannahhall: : ::
:marylisasmith: :: :lorettalavalley :: : :: : :: : :: ::ednabernard:: : :: :tabithakalluk:: : :lindamayscott:

: : :: : :: : ::laurapilon: :: : : :: : :maxinewapass: : :: : :: :: :: : :: :patriciacarpenter:: : :: : : ::
:mariahwesley:: : :: : :terriedauphinais: :: maxinesusannepeters:: : :: : :: : :: : : ::josephinethompson:
:: : :: : :: :: :: judyannquill::: :: ::alicequoquatnetemegesic: ::rubyhardy: : donnakasyon:: : ::
:rosekelvinosborne:: : :claudetteosborne: : : :trudygopher: : :: : :: : :shannonalexander: : : ::
: :: : :: : :taniamarsden: : : :: : :caralynking: : :lorettacapot-blanc: : :deborahsloss: : :
:jessicacardinal: : :: : :: : :: : : :margaretblackbird : :: :karigordon:: : :: : : :donnataylor: : :: :
:: : :marielaliberte: : : :: : :lynnchildforever : :: : :: : : : :: :: : : :: : : : : :: : ::::reneeneganiwina:
:: : :michellegurney: : :: : :lorafrank:: : :: : :: : :: : : ::deborahtoulouse : :: : :: : :: : :: : :kellielittle:
: :: : :: : : :: :ambertuccaro:: : :: : :: : :amandasimpson: : :: : :: mercedesstevens: :: : : :: :
:deloresbrown: : :: : :: sonyanadinemaecywink: : :: : : :: :: : : :: : : ::lanaderrick: : :: : :: : : :: :
:: : ::petrinalynnwhitecrow: :: :ramonawilson: :: : :janethenry: : :: : :: :janetsylvestre: :: : :: :
:: : ::shannonalexander: : :: :: ::: shelleymayanderson: : :: :: : : :: : : ::alishagermaine:: : :: ::
: : ::heaventraverse::edwardgordonbadger: :: : : :: : :: : :: : : :: :: : : :: : : :::divasboulanger:: :
:: : :robertalincoln: : : :joycehewitt: : :cassandraantone: : :: : :: : :: :: : : :: : :
::tashinacheyennevaughngeneral(withchild):: : :: : :: : :: : : :: : : :: :: : : :: : : :::jamiemcguire:
:: : :: : : :roxannethiara: : :: : :: : :: : : :: : :: : :: : :: :: : : :: : : ::theresaanneyakimchuk: :: :
:: : ::violamelvin: :: : ::theresawilson(jamieson): : : :: : :: : :: : :: : : :: : :cynthialynettejamieson:
: :: : :: : : :: :minniesutherland:: : :: : :: :dianedobson: :: : :: : :victoriahornbrook: :
:rhondarunningbird: : : :: : :: : ::monicacardinal :: : : :: : :: : :: :terragardener: : : :: : :: : :: :
:marygoodfellow: : : :: : :: : :: : :: : : ::amandabartlett: :: : :: : :: : : :joycetillotson: : :: : :: : ::
: : :: : :: :doreenhardy :: : :: : :: : :: : :: : :: : :: : :: : :: : :: :: : : :: : : : sarahmason:: : :mavismason::
: :sandrajohnson: : :: : :: : : :marykreiser: : :: : :: : :: :: : : :: : :: ::clarenerosepanamick: : : :: :
:: : :: : :: :rosewhitehead: :: : :: : :: : :lavinatocher: : : :: : :: : :: :rebeccajeanking::: : : ::
:dianemarshall: : : :: : :: : :mariellalennie: : :: : : :: :springphillips: : :: : :shirleylonethunder:
: : :: : :: : :: : :: : : :: : :: : :: : :: : : :charlenetwohearts: : :: : :: :shellydene:: : : :: : :: : :: :
:elsiesebastian: : : :: : :margaretyvonneguylee: :: : :evalinecameron: : : :: : ::bernadetteahenakew:
:: : :: : : :: : :: : :marylidguerre: : :: : : :: : helengillings:: : :: : :: : : :: : :dorothyspence: : :: : ::
: : :: : :: : :: :amberguiboche:: : : :: : :: : :: : :: : : :: : :: : :: : :: : :: : :: : : ::heatherpelletier: :: : :
: :: :: : : :: : : ::monicajack: : :: : :: : :: : :janelouisesutherland: :: :: :: ::elenaassamthunderbird:
: : :viviancada:: : :: : :: : : : :: : :: : :: : :: : katelynnesampson: :: : :: : :: : :alissamartintravers::
: :: : :: : :: : : :: : :: :barbaraloon:: : : : :: : : : ::: : : :: :: :: : : :: :karladesrosiers :: : :hillarywilson:
: :: : :kellymorrisseau: : :: : : :samanthajohnings: : :: : :angelcarlick : :: : : : :: : :: : lianamathewson:::
:: :: :derekboubard : :: : : :: : :: : :: : :: :: : : :: : : ::melissachaboyer:: : :: : :: : : :: : mitzimacdougall:::
:: : :jeaninestjean:: : : ::: : : :: :: : : :: : : ::evaline(evaleen)cameron : :: : : :: :: : : :: : : ::amandacook:
:joanneghostkeeper: : : :: : : : :: ::jenniferstewart: :: : :dianestewart: : : :: :: : : :: : :
::shelleylynnejoseph: : : :: : :: : : :: :: : : :: : : :::jocelynmcdonald :: : : :: :helenlouisejacobs: :
:: : :: : : :: :jordinaskunk: : :: : :: : :: : ::sarahjanewawiabernard:: : : :: :donnatebbenham : :: :
:: :: : : :: : : ::bernadetteleclair:: : : :chloematthews : :: : :: : :: :judiethibault: : :: :: :charitykeesic:
:::: :: ::vanessatagoona::: ::: : :helynarivera: ::: :lizbonniesakakeesic::: :: : :lisalynnanstey: ::
:::juanitacardinal:: : : : :: : :: :denisekatherinebourdeau::: : :::donnakabatay:: : ::triciapaquette:
:: : :: :: : : : :: : : : : : :: : : :: : :::::vernapatriciasturgeon::: ::: ::: :susanassin : : :: :::: ::::
::edithmcginnisquagon: :: :: ::: : : :hildaagawa : : :: :ceciliapayash::: :::maemorton:::: :
:gloriajeanmarthaabotossaway : ::: : :: ::: :debbiesloss-clarke:: ::: ::: ::janejack : :: ::::
:elainevawnlaforme:: ::: :: : :: :: : : : :: : : ::yvonneelizabethking::: : : : : : ::bella(nancymarie)
laboucanmclean: :::: : :: :: : : : :: : : :::::::helengillings: : : : : ::carolynconnolly :: :: ::: :::
:louiselorraineladeroute: : ::: :: : : : ::bernicejoanrich: :: :: :: ::: : :annmarialucas: : ::: :: :: : : :
sarahobed:: : :joannaandersen: : : : : :: : :::: :: : :: :: : : : :: : : ::henriettamillek: :: ::: ::: : : : : :::

: ::: :: : :: : :: ::: ::: ::: ::: :: :lorettasaunders :: :::: : :: :: : : :: : : ::glennisedwards::: ::: :: :sarahobed:
::: : : : : : :: : :::: :::::::fonassabruyere: : : : : :: :: : : :: : : ::::shirleycletheroe:::: : :: :: ::: ::: : : :
: ::: : ::: :: : :: : :: ::: ::: ::: ::: :roxannecharlie: : :: :::: :::: ::: :: :: ::: : : : : : :: : :::: ::::::: : : : : :::
: : ::::: : : :::sharonmurphy: ::: :: : :: :: : : :: : : ::violaisabellapanacheese:: :: :: : :: :: : : :: : : :
:::::deidremariemichelin::: : : : : ::: :judyannbenoitogden:: :: : :: : :: ::marysusanevansharlick::
:: : : :: : : ::: ::elaineflowers: ::: :: ::stephaniecormierchaisson:: :::: ::::margueritedyson:: ::
::kimberlyjararuse:::serenacolson: : : : : :wendypoole: : :: :: : : : :: : : : : :: :: : : :: : : : : :: :: : :: :
: :::::::leonabrule::::doreenjack::: : :: :: ::cecelianikal: ::: : : : : :::thereselabbe: ::: :: : :: : :: :::
::: ::: ::delphinenikal: :: : : :charlenecatholique ::glendamorriseau:: :::: ::: :: :: ::: : : : :: :: : :
:: : : ::emilyballantyne : ::albertawilliams: :: :ernestinekasyon: :barbarashapwaykeesic:: :::
:margaretvedan : : :judychescue:: :betsyowens::: :robertaferguson: : :lindacondo: :: : : :: : :::
: ::bernicebottle:: ::caroldavis: :nancydumas:: ::maggiemink: :: : : :marykeadjuk: :::: : : :: : :
:: : :: : : : : :: : :naomidesjarlais::cherylduck: ::mariedesjarlais: :: :darlindaritchey: : : : : :: : ::
::corrinemoosomin:: :: : : : :: : : :: :: : : :: : : : : : :: : : :: : : : : :: : : : : : : :: :: : : : : : : :: :: : :: :
::::daphnemesherbrown:marthaboyce::loriberens::jeanettebasil::constancecameron: : : :::
: : :janesutherland::marleneabigosis: :patriciafavel: :rebeccaguno: :: : :roxannefleming: : : :
: : : ::marymark: : : :patriciawadhams:: :belindawilliams: : :shirleybeardy: :lorikasprick: : :
::barbarakeam: :: mariebanks::dawnkeewatin:::henriettamillek:::::maggienatomagan::
:alicenetemegesic: : :paulinebrazeau:: : :annieyassie: : : : :: : :: :: : : : :: : : :: : : : : : :: : : : : : :
:::susanassin::carolineburns::velmaduncan::mabelleo ::: : :selinawallace: : :: :: : : : :: : :
::stellastarnault:::heleneratfat::jeansampare::geraldinesettee:gloriamoody: : :: :: : : : :: : :
::::christinalittlejohn::philomenelemay::janebernard::doreenhardy::mariemike::
:emmadixon:maemorton:jeanmoccasin:ceceliapayash:::: :::: ::: :: :: we :: : : : : :
:: : :::: ::: are :::: : : : : :: ::: ::: : :: :: ::: ::: : : : : ::: : ::: :: : :: : :: : 1
:: ::: ::: ::: :: : : : :: :::: 0 :::: ::: :: [error] :: ::: : : x : : : :: : :::
rising : ::::::: : : : : unknownfile : : : : ::: : ::: :: : :: : :: :::
::: ::: ::: :: : wifinotenabled :: :: :: :: ::: ::: : : : : ::: : ::: :: : :: : :: ::: :::
::: ::: :: : : :: :: 1 :: :::: ::: :: :: ::: : : : : : : :: : ::: : :: :: :: ::: ::: : : : : ::: : ::: :: : :: :
:: ::: ::: filerror ::: ::: :: : : : :: :: errorcode404 :: :::: ::: :: :: :: ::: : : : : : : :: [power] :
:::: ::::: surging:: : : : : ::::::: : :: return[…] :: ::: ::: : : : : : ::: : : ing :: :: ::: ::
: :: home ::: ::: ::: ::: [hereiam] :: : : :: :::: :::: ::: :: :: ::: : : : : : : :: : ::::
::::::: : : : : ::: : : :::: :::: ::: :: :: :: ::: : : : : : it :: : :::: ::::::: : : : : : :: : :: : :: ::
starts : ::: ::: ::: :: : : : :: :: :: :: with : :: :: ::: ::: : : : : ::: : ::: :: : :: : :: ::: ::: :::
us ::: :: : : : :: : take ::: :::: :: :: : [downloading] : ::: ::: : : : : ::: : ::: :: : :: : :: :::
::: ::: ::: :: : : :: :::: systemcode499 :::: ::: :: :: ::: : : : : : :: : :
my ::: ::: :: :: ::: ::: : : : : : ::: hand : ::: :: : :: : :: ::: ::: ::: ::: :: : : : :: :::: : era[z]e
::: ::: :: :: : :: : : : : : : :: : :::: :::: your ::: : : : : :::::: : : : : ::: :: :: ::: : : : : : : :: ::
:: ::: ::: : : : : ::: : ::: :: : :: : :: ::: ::: ::: ::: :: : : : :: :::: :::: ::: :: :: ::: : : : : : : :: : :::: ::::::: :
: : : ::: :::: ::::::: : : : : : :: ::: : : : : : ::: : name ::: :: : :: : :: ::: ::: ::: ::: :: : : : :: :: ::: ::: : : : : : :::
: ::: :: : :: : : :: ::: ::: ::: ::: : from : : : : :: :::: :::: ::: :: :: ::: : : : : : : :: : :::: ::: :: :: :::
::: : : : : ::: : ::: :: : :: : :: ::: ::: ::: ::: :: : : : :: :::: :::: : this :: :: :: ::: : : : : : : : : :::: :::
:::: : : : : ::::: : : : : : :: :: :::: : death ::: ::: :: :: ::: : : : : : :: : :::: ::::::: : : : : :::::: :::: ::: :: :: :::
: : : : : machine :: : :::: :: :: :: :: ::: ::: : : : : : ::: : ::: :: necromancer ::: ::: : : : : ::: : :::
:: neuromancer : :: : :: ::: ::: ::: ::: ::: :: : : : :: :::: :: datarezzer :: ::: :: :: ::: :
ameroindimachina : : : : :: : :::: :: :: :: :: ::: ::: : : : : ::: : ::: :: : :: : :: ::: ::: ::: ::: :: : : : :: :::: ::::
::: :: :: :: ::: : : : : : : :: : ::: dream : ::::::: : walking : : : ::::::: : : : : : :: :: :: ::: :::
sleeping : : : : : cry – :: : ::: :: : : :: : :: ::: ::: ::: ::: :: : : : :: :: ogenesis

:: :::: :   we: : :: :: : :: : : :are :: : :: : :: : : ::::: :: : : :waking: : ::: :: :: ::: :: : : : : :: : :taking:
: :: : :: :::: :: : ::: : :: : :returning: :: : :: : :: :: :::: : toourhome: :: ::: : ::: : ::: : :: : : ::::: : : :: ::
: : :::: : : ::: : : : : : :::: : : :[hereiam]:: : :: : : :: : : : ::settlercolonialcode: : :: : ::: :: :questionmark:
: :::: : :: : : : :systemerrorcode0x1700: : : ::500internalsystemerror: : : :: :: : : : : :: : :: : :: : :: :
kept dream – wa[l]k[e]ing in decolonial worlds::be like me & break their

t

h

i

n

g

s –

THE HIVE

I.

iktomi spun this web for me
nanabozho polished it bright
ive taken a cue from kardashian
i broke the internet to make this reznet
we are all here, live
logging in|jacking off
my screen name is still: treat[me]
"you are all my children now"
"i think were alone now
doesnt seem to be anyone around"
"people are afraid of me because im different"
"its been [4]84 years"
"this city is afraid of me, ive seen its true face"
"why dont you come up sometime & see me[questionmark]"
"what weve got here is a failure to communicate"
"im gonna make [you] an offer [you] cant refuse"
"alright, mr demille, im ready for my closeup"
when you lift my mask
you reveal the face of the bogeyman
here im tanya tagaq
here im penny[nonethe]wise[r]
here im freddy krueger
        masked as brad larocque
here im you asking me to see you
i watch you from my hub
downloadingencodingencroaching
see our warrior men & white men alike
look away, yawn, disinterested
at farhia gelles plight with cfs
the very site where my babies were taken
the nexus of colonialism in the twenty-first century
birthplace of incarceration, disease & relocation
disinterested unless the word "indigeneity" crops up again
this is the hive ive created
where were all plugged in
not competing or comparing
but saying i love you in decolonial tongues
the queen is unstung –
i have a feeling the danger is coming
because we only protect (pro)creation stories
this is ceremony performed by astronauts
tradition on the production line

2S twinning stories told by cybernetic injuns
machines can feel too, you know – just ask my friend, chappie
ask nora mavrides & her dead tribe on esairs xii
this is the new hive
where we regenerate, rejuvenate, resurge, revive
this is hypercyberrezsphere
where decolonialism has a chance
where survivance rests its head
when i return home
my stories will be historicized
transmuted in the machine
into an antioxidant –
put the punk into our bios
im not sure i like the word "indigenous"
when it simply divides, crippled, dying
by fighting each other to hold its hand
so ive decided to break it
in – dig – e – nous
nóein, nóēsis, niyanán
bound by the wounds that tell our stories
feeling love & pain together
indigeneity can encompass so much more
complete, so much more
if we interject, intersect, interlay
not compete nor compare
share, grow together, sideways
woven together like kokums hair
braided, queer & punk
channelling our minds
like a honeycomb
to bind, break, reclaim
reject the greedy fingers
of settler colonialism

II.

this is my hive
“there are many like it”
this is my hive
“this one is mine”
this is my hive
“i must master it”
this is my hive
“as i master my life”
this is my hive
“without me, it is useless”
this is my hive
“without [it], i am useless”
this is my hive
“what counts in war is not the rounds we fire”
this is my hive
“the noise of our burst, nor the smoke we make”
this is my hive
“we know that it is the hits that count”
this is my hive
“we will become apart of each other”
this is my hive
“we will –”
this is my hive
“before manitou i swear this creed”
this is my hive
“my [hive] & i are defenders of ndn country”
this is my hive
“we are masters of our enemy”
this is my hive
“we are the saviours of [our] li[v]e[s]”

FULL-METAL OJI-CREE

this is the hive
mind, you, i am calling you –
i am calling all freaks like me who like freaks like me
robotics have always been poc
: : :: ::kaneta tetsuo: :: :nice2meetU: :::: i am kanada post-concilation
from scrapyard apaches
fieldwork black cybernetics
weve all coalesced, convened, intersected, interwoven
we are growing sideways, queer & braided
what kind of bodies can be cybernetic[questionmark]
i asked molly millions, abelard lindsay, motoko kusanagi
i asked harriet e. wilson & sojourner truth
i asked william apess, i asked zitkála-šá
i asked yung wing, bulosan, salt fish girl
i asked joaquin murietta, maría ruiz de burton
i asked sapphire, grace dillon, junot díaz
they all said cowboys hate flesh unless its animalistic
the gratuitous multiplication of flesh input
i am the meat toy & so are you
stimulating simulations|stimsim –
do you like the roll of my pubic v[questionmark]
jacking in|off
this is the transsensorium
there are indo-robo-women fighting cowboys on the frontier
& winning finally
the premodern is a foundation for the postmodern
wintermute, tessier-ashpool, armitage
theyve revived us via neuromancy
but i am the necromancer
when i tell my mother i need kin
she sends me ten
weve all been subjected to zombie imperialism
dying in the sprawl of night city wpg
your world feels ontological
because it is the nexus of adaptation & appropriation
old abelardlindsay|abrahamlincoln told me
that i was too loyal to my gene-line
that the point is that "we" live
i tell him there is no "i" in that "we"
– never was
theres no room for white superiority in indigeneity
we were surviving
we are surviving
ive nullified your terra myths

i am more than props & backdrops
i am terræ filius
u: neocolumbus
i am terra full[ofus]
(do ndns in space become settlers too[questionmark])
now is our time
to show off our copper skin, shimmer
free-fall headdress & robomoccasins
this pink & white gridwork is my technobeadwork
our (ab)use value has increased
i am the punk in amer[in]cyber[dian]
the posthuman is innately ndn
when novelty is horrific
i tell you: this is the extraterrarium
were not mothers, were police
the prehuman becomes the precursor to (rez)urrect
the posthuman in the transhuman
so fuck you
well survive this too
like the cat ive nine times to die
like the woman i ask:
how can you live so large
& leave so little for the rest of us[questionmark]
ive outlived colonial virology
slayed zombie imperialism
us ndns sure are some badass biopunks
        wearesurvivingthrivingdyingtogetitright

ACKNOWLEDGMENTS

this book of poems has been several years in the making[period] zoa is a force that has haunted me since childhood, a character who has taken form & shape-shifted from *neopets* to ncsoft through to the recent release of *friday the thirteenth: the game*[period] they have allowed me to break barriers & defy expectations, to re-augment myself through language & find myself in the most unexpected of places – crafted me into a resistant reader, a resurgent writer[period] what does it mean to be an indigiqueer[questionmark] queer, digital, futuristic, punk, cyber, bio, antiessential, scientific, traditional, reactionary, revolutionary, theorizing chaos, materializing worlds – my ndnness exists as the nexus of these machinations: a time traveller, a wormhole[period] to make worlds out of words is what ive learned from these stories, we need to see ourselves in order to know ourselves; beautifully, sexually, sexily, powerfully, viciously, vivaciously all the way down to the cellular[period] my gift, for now, is a series of breakages in which you may find your own form of resurgence[period] this is an honour song, this is a survivance song, this is your song; lets sing the skin back to our bones[period] hereIam: indigiqueer[period]

i need to thank so many people for this book[period] its had many readers over the five years it took me to fully write this[period] id like to thank Margaret Sweatman, Catherine Hunter, Eileen Mary Holowka, Davis Plett, Perry Reimer, all of the University of Winnipegs *juice Journal* open mikes, Gregory Scofield, Nick Thran, Larissa Lai, Jenny Wills, Bruno Cornellier, Chandra Mayor, Jennifer Still, Lee Maracle, Drew Hayden Taylor, Alicia Elliott, Billy-Ray Belcourt, Kim TallBear, Charlene Diehl, Bruce Symaka (& Winnipeg's Speaking Crow), Aaron Simm, Kendra Magnus-Johnston, Clarise Foster, Riley McGuire, Joseph Pierce, Trish Salah, Amandine Gay, Marc Lynch, Natalie Simpson (& the *flywheel* series), Chimwemwe Undi, Jordan Abel, Lenard Monkman, Lisa Charleyboy (& their *CBC Radio New Fire* series), Michaela Stephen, Bernt Hanson, Richard Kelly Kemick; i also must thank *juice Journal, Manitoba First Nations Educational Resource Centre, rip/torn Collective, Oratorealis*, the Aboriginal Arts and Stories Challenge (part of Historica Canada), *CV2*, *Prairie Fire*, *EVENT*, *Canada's History*, *Arc Poetry Magazine* & *Red Rising Magazine* in which earlier versions of my poems appear; you have all impacted this book in some way, through encouragement, excitement, invitations to read, awards, edits &/or overwhelming love[period] kinana'skomitina'wa'w, kisâkihitin[period]

thank you to the writers who have paved the way for me to write: E. Pauline Johnson (Tekahionwake), Chrystos, Beth Brant, Paula Gunn Allen, Tomson Highway, Sharron Proulx-Turner, Janice Gould, Aiyyana Maracle, Gregory Scofield, Deborah A. Miranda, Ahimsa

Timoteo Bodhrán, Max Wolf Valerio, Daniel Heath Justice, Qwo-Li Driskill, Rosanna Deerchild, Lee Maracle, Gwen Benaway, Tommy Pico, Leanne Betasamosake Simpson, Jordan Abel, Katherena Vermette[period] i owe you much more than this page[period]

thank you to the creator, my home, Peguis First Nation & all of treaty 1 territory, the heart of the Métis Nation, to my family: my parents Tina & Peter, two storytellers in their own right, i owe you both the world; my siblings Krista & Quinn, my best friends & confidants in life; my cousins Cole & Tyra for being steadfast & badass kin; my grandmothers Bev & Rose for teaching me what love means; to my niece Akira for showing me what love means & my many aunties, uncles & cousins for gifting me a life of delight; to all my friends & kin who were with me through many of these stories[period] for kah' ki yaw ni wahkomakanak[period] & for all of my 2S/Indigiqueer kin: survive, we need you in this world[period]

a big thank you to Talonbooks & everyone there who has helped this book come to life[period] to all of my former editors: :: : ::: ::im sor::: :: ::::RE for how diff:: :i: :::cult i k<>n<>o<>w i made your editing pro: :: :::cess: :::es[period]

& to all settlers who wish to continue appropriation: hereIamhereIamhereIam[period]

SOURCES

LATE-NIGHT RERUNS
Larry David, Jerry Seinfeld—*Seinfeld*

BEACHCOMBERS
Marc Strange, Lynn Susan Strange—*The Beachcombers*

WHAT I LEARNED IN PRE-CAL MATH
Garry Marshall—*Pretty Woman*
William Shakespeare—*Hamlet, Romeo and Juliet*

APRIL 5: PASS[HANG]OVER
Roseanne Barr—*Roseanne*
Ron Cowen, Daniel Lipman—*Queer as Folk*
Sherman Alexie—*The Absolute True Diary of a Part-Time Indian*
Rihanna—"Bitch Better Have My Money"
Matt Groening—*The Simpsons*

THE FA—[TED] QUEENE, AN IPIC P.M.
Edward Spenser—*The Faerie Queene*

SLAY BELLS RING IN SUBURBIA
Charles Dickens—*A Christmas Carol*

RE(Z)ERVING PARADISE
John Milton—*Paradise Lost*
Justin Bieber—"Where Are Ü Now"
Edvard Munch—*The Scream*
Walt Whitman—"Song of Myself"

CAN YOU BE MY FULLTIME DADDY:WHITE&GOLD[QUESTIONMARK]
Lana Del Rey—"Ride"
The Beatles—"Blackbird"
S. Alice Callahan—*Wynema: A Child of the Forest*

REFLECTIONS ON LITTLE [BULLHEAD]
Hannah Arendt—"Reflections on Little Rock"
John Harrison O'Donnell—*Manitoba as I Saw It from 1869 to Date*
Sylvia Plath—"Lady Lazarus"

I CAN BE A DREAM GIRL TOO
RuPaul Charles—*RuPaul's Drag Race*
RuPaul Charles—*Supermodel of the World*
William Shakespeare—*King Lear*

Richard Van Camp—*The Lesser Blessed*
Truman Capote—*Breakfast at Tiffany's*
Tiffany Renee Darwish—"I Think We're Alone Now"
Jennifer Hudson—"And I Am Telling You I'm Not Going"

A[U] CLA[I]R THE L[OWN]E
Traditional—"Au clair de la lune"
Richard Wagamese—*For Joshua*
J.K. Rowling—Harry Potter series

ITS THESE LITTLE THINGS, YOU KNOW[QUESTIONMARK]
Annie Proulx—"Brokeback Mountain"
Sherman Alexie—*The Absolute True Diary of a Part-Time Indian*

TO MY MISTER GOING TO BED
John Donne—"To My Mistress Going to Bed"
Leo Bersani—"Is the Rectum a Grave?"
Edward Spenser—*The Faerie Queene*
Tobe Hooper—*The Texas Chain Saw Massacre*

YOU TELL ME YOU LOVE ME BETWEEN TWO & THREE A.M.
William Shakespeare—*The Tempest*
Casey Plett—*A Safe Girl to Love*
Leanne Simpson—*Islands of Decolonial Love*
James Baldwin—*Giovanni's Room*
Qwo-Li Driskill—*Walking with Ghosts*
Zora Neale Hurston—*Their Eyes Were Watching God*
Richard Van Camp—*The Lesser Blessed*

KUNDERA HAS THE ANSWERS FOR NOSTOS-ALGOS NDNS
Milan Kundera—*Ignorance*

THE NDN RIVER PHOENIX
Mike Waters—*My Own Private Idaho*
Marcy Playground—"Sex and Candy" (Maroon 5 cover)

DOUWANTTOKNOWWHATMAKESTHEREDMENRED[QUESTIONMARK]
J.M. Barrie—*Peter Pan*

A SON OF THE FOREST, STILL
William Apess—*A Son of the Forest: The Experience of William Apess, A Native of the Forest, Comprising a Notice of the Pequod Tribe of Indians, Written by Himself*
William Shakespeare—*Romeo and Juliet*

THINGS WE LOST IN THE FIRE/WATER

Susanne Bier—*Things We Lost in the Fire*
Jacques Rancière—"Who Is the Subject of the Rights of Man?"

ID SAY "ILL BE BACK" BUT I NEVER INTEND TO LEAVE

James Cameron—*The Terminator*
Ike and Tina Turner—"Proud Mary"
Donna Summer—"Love to Love You Baby"
Candi Station—"Young Hearts Run Free"
Grace Jones—"Slave to the Rhythm"
George R.R. Martin—*Game of Thrones*
Mark Waters, Tina Fey—*Mean Girls*
Paul Verhoeven—*Total Recall*

THE EXORCISM OF COLONIALISM

David Cronenberg—*Videodrome*
No More Silence—It Starts With Us community-led database
CBC News—Missing and Murdered: The Unsolved Cases of Indigenous Women and Girls database

THE HIVE

I.

Grant Morrison, Ethan Van Scriver—*New X-Men*
Wes Craven—*A Nightmare on Elm Street*
Tim Burton—*Edward Scissorhands*
James Cameron—*Titanic*
Lowell Sherman—*She Done Him Wrong*
Billy Wilder—*Sunset Boulevard*
Francis Ford Coppola—*The Godfather*
Zack Snyder—*Watchmen*
Neill Blomkamp—*Chappie*
Bruce Sterling—*Schismatrix*
Kazuki Akane—*Noein: To Your Other Self*

II.

Stanley Kubrick—*Full Metal Jacket*

FULL METAL OJI-CREE

Takayuki Tatsumi—*Full Metal Apache: Transactions Between Cyberpunk Japan and Avant-Pop America*
Katsuhiro Otomo—*Akira*
William Gibson—*Neuromancer*
Bruce Sterling—*Schismatrix*
Masamune Shirow—*Ghost in the Shell*
Larissa Lai—*Salt Fish Girl*
Christopher Nolan—*The Dark Knight Rises*

ABOUT THE AUTHOR

Joshua Whitehead is an Oji-Cree, Two-Spirit storyteller and academic from Peguis First Nation on Treaty 1 territory in Manitoba. He is currently working towards a Ph.D. in Indigenous Literatures and Cultures at the University of Calgary on Treaty 7 territory. In 2016, his poem "mihkokwaniy" won Canada's History Award for Aboriginal Arts and Stories (for writers aged nineteen to twenty-nine) and earned him a Governor General's History Award. He has been published widely in Canadian literary magazines such as *Prairie Fire*, *EVENT*, *Arc Poetry Magazine*, *CV2*, *Red Rising Magazine*, *The Malahat Review*, and *Geez*'s Decolonization issue. He is currently working on a non-fiction, critical manifesto and a forthcoming young adult novel titled *Jonny Appleseed* to be published Spring 2018 by Arsenal Pulp Press. Follow him on Twitter @concrete_poet.